The Peaceable Sex

ON AGGRESSION IN
WOMEN AND MEN

Margarete Mitscherlich, M.D.

Translated from the German by

CRAIG TOMLINSON

Fromm International Publishing Corporation

NEW YORK

*The translator wishes to thank Beverley R. Placzek for her
careful review of the manuscript and her many contributions thereto.*

Designed by Constance Fogler
Printed in the United States of America
First U.S. Edition

Library of Congress Cataloging-in-Publication Data

Mitscherlich, Margarete.
The peaceable sex.

Translation of: Die friedfertige Frau.
Bibliography: p. 229
Includes index.
1. Aggressiveness (Psychology) 2. Men—Psychology.
3. Women—Psychology. 4. Women—Attitudes.
5. Psychoanalysis. I. Title.
BF575.A3M5513 1987   302.5′4   87-289
ISBN 0-88064-067-7

Contents

FOREWORD

War and Violence–
Men's Business?

IN ALL historical epochs, wars have been fought by men.
Men have prepared, planned, and carried out wars; they
have exterminated opposing armies; they have taken pris-
oners (or taken none); they have laid waste to entire tracts
of land; they have conquered continents, "colonialized"
and extinguished cultures, and they have slaughtered
women, children, and elderly people in the process.

Men have invented and manufactured the instruments
of warfare. They have created an entire profession, that
of the warrior and soldier; they have invented a weapons
industry with its own doctrine, professional examinations,
its own morality, ranks, and hierarchies.

In all epochs known to us, there have been wars: small
wars, large wars, guerrilla wars, and general wars—all
fought exclusively by men. Recent times have seen gen-
ocide, human and technological conflagrations resulting
in millions of dead and wounded, cities razed and land-
scapes torn apart, whole populations uprooted.

Throughout history, it has been primarily men who have

committed violent crimes. They have beaten and stabbed, shot and dismembered, tortured and raped, burned and broken on the wheel, strangled and garrotted—and they have invented and refined the instruments used for these acts of violence. They have invented entire industries of brutality, each with its own specialists and researchers.

During all this time, women have served and supported the men, following the warriors and attending to their physical well-being—in bed and in the kitchen, in field hospitals and bordellos. They have almost always been victimized: either they were being raped, tortured, murdered, enslaved, or treated as the spoils of war; or they were mourning the head of the family or their children. In the industry of violence as well, women have played a subordinate role: They operate machines, take care of office work, staff the canteens. Only rarely have women imitated the men; only rarely has it been possible to induce them to take part directly in the "horrors of war."

Men's aggression and inclination to violence have been the object of scholarly studies time and again. Biological, social, cultural, anthropological, political, and psychological theories, as well as philosophical systems, have been developed in order to explain aggression and violence. People have fantasized and speculated, and the calls and appeals to reform the aggressors and to do away with violence and war have been legion.

All of the great religions and philosophers have advocated nonviolence, philanthropy, love, friendship, and community. All psychologists, too, pursue the goal of making people less violent, of increasing understanding, mutual respect, and love—so far without the slightest success. Wars become more and more horrible and ruthless all the time, and people—not only in war—more violent and beastly. Those of our pessimistic contemporaries who are susceptible to thoughts of annihilation are understandably coming to the conclusion that men, who have dominated world history, carry within them an unalterable, evolutionarily developed death drive, an apparatus of destruction that forces them to undo with one hand everything that they have built with the other, with the aim of finally destroying themselves and the entire globe.

Is it conceivable that one half of the human species, men, are inherently subject to destructive inclinations that cannot be sated short of self-extermination, and that the other half of the species, women, are less at the mercy of such inclinations, and, moreover, are condemned to submit passively to the destructive intentions of others, whether as servant, as victim, or as forced accomplice? Is it possible that only one half of humanity has destructive inclinations, and that the other does not? Must not both have such inclinations? And if they do, what does the other half—women—do with these inclinations, how do they work them through? How do they prevent them from operating with such destructive results, for themselves and others, as they do in men? Can the approach and attitudes toward violence and destruction that women have developed over the course of history, more or less of necessity, serve as a model for a less destructive management of aggression?

These and related questions will be investigated in this book's various chapters, which are based on papers written at various times and for various occasions. All have been thoroughly revised; all share the common theme of the origins and consequences of male and female aggression. The essays are meant only as a stimulus. Answers and definitive statements should not be expected of them; the subject is too complex for that. Just as thus far no one has been able to provide us with any answers, or with practicable suggestions for change, this book, too, will not expect to do more than to provide a stimulus for thought and to convey insights into types of behavior and ways of thinking that we often find incomprehensible. If these attempts can serve to stimulate further questions and research, if they make women reflect on their powers and abilities—and use them—they will have fulfilled their purpose.

It remains for me to convey my sincere gratitude to Marieluise von Schweinichen for her tireless efforts and patience in the preparation of the manuscript. Without the energetic assistance of Willi Köhler, for which I am most grateful, the papers on which this book is based would probably still be lying in my desk drawer. I would also like to thank Ingeborg Pabel for correcting the manuscript and preparing the bibliography.

The Peaceable Sex

I

Women and Aggression–
An Overview

IN A TIME when "women for peace" has become something of a slogan, writing about women and their aggression or lack of it can engender false expectations. I would like to make clear at the outset that by aggression I do not mean male violence, and by lack of aggression I do not mean female passivity.

I will consider the complex development of aggression and its gender-specific forms of expression only in broad outlines. Sometimes, however, such an overview of potential explanations provides a better orientation than could a more detailed (but nonetheless cursory) treatment of the variety of problems and theories involved. In so doing, it is sometimes impossible to avoid generalizations and oversimplifications.

Before turning to psychoanalysis, my own discipline, I would like to discuss several problems of the present and the immediate past from a psychological point of view. Many of our contemporaries regard the threat of nuclear warfare as *the* aggression-related problem. Even so, this

3

danger is often perceived only intellectually, without a corresponding level of anxiety. It would be senseless, according to some, to concern oneself with a threat against which one is powerless anyway. In their view, participation in the struggle against nuclear destruction, with the constant parading before our eyes of the horrors that lie in store for us, would only serve the purpose of masochistic gratification. It is much more sensible, according to such people, to attend to the pressing social problems in our immediate environment. This sounds quite reasonable, but if we were to examine our contemporaries more closely, we would discover that, with the help of one worry, one anxiety, another is clearly being repressed and denied. The emphasis placed on current worries and needs serves to repress thoughts of unimaginable destruction in the future and, frequently, of past crimes as well.

Exclusive interest in the peace movement, on the other hand, can cause us to lose sight of the injustices and social problems of the present. As has already been noted, an awareness of one danger can be combined with forgetting and repressing another.

In the women's movement, too, the question of how the theme of peace might relate to the situation of women has often been discussed. Few women can imagine themselves joining a military combat force or calling for increased rearmament; on the other hand, women have wondered whether in allying themselves with "women for peace" they were not allowing themselves to revert to their former roles as accommodating, mediating, subservient women. "Peace" can also become the stifling peace of an uncritical and passive acceptance of habitual injustices, such as those that women have long had forced upon them.

From a psychological point of view, the threat of war is always accompanied by a division of people into camps of good and bad, that is, by the projection of repressed portions of an individual's own mental life onto perceived enemies. Thus the situation is rationalized as follows: "It is the evil foreigners who threaten us, and not the possibility of a cataclysmic nuclear war." Without projection and without displacement of guilt by both sides, the mentality of war and the arms race would be inconceivable. That such attitudes may be observed more frequently in men than in women is a theme to which I shall later return.

I would like to begin by focusing on the history of the student protests during the late 1960s and on the revitalization of the women's movement and its psychological underpinnings, in order to better understand the current situation and to avoid the amnesia so apparent today. The student protests represented a generational conflict; in West Germany, at least, the protest centered on a conflict with fathers and their pasts. Following the war, that parental generation had increasingly identified itself politically with the United States and had idealized it, supporting that superpower's military actions rather uncritically. Thus the protests were triggered not only by repression of the Nazi past but also by the Vietnam War, by contemporaneous circumstances in Iran, by late imperialist behavior toward the Third World, and much more.

The deidealization of Americans in Germany was accompanied by a deidealization of parents, above all of the father, that had been previously in the making but had not been clearly expressed until that time. For the first time, a large number of young people, not merely isolated individuals, took an interest in the events that took place during the Third Reich and the consequences of those events. Their parents' past became a focal point of their interest. Here as well, however, one could not help observing a displacement of guilt: Our generation—the younger—is innocent and capable of critical thought, while yours—the older—is guilty and incapable of questioning itself.

This conflict occurred primarily between fathers and sons or their substitutes. It was a conflict between men, and showed once again that tendency toward projection that, in my view, is particularly characteristic of the manner in which men deal with their aggressions—that is, by seeking and finding scapegoats.

At the same time, the women's movement was reinvigorated. This was all the more astounding inasmuch as patriarchal relations were the status quo in student affairs. Women were treated no differently by their student peers than by society at large.

A glance at the history of the women's movement shows that it ceased to exist during the Nazi reign. In Nazi ideology, women's existence was justified only by their role as mothers, preferably mothers of sons, although women proved useful in armaments factories during the war. But, to a large extent, it was women who assumed responsibility in the home during and just after the Second World War, when the men were either fighting or held prisoner; women contributed substantially to making the reconstruction of Germany possible in the first place. In the mens' absence, they had learned to care for themselves as well as for their children.

During the first years after the war, many German women refused to subjugate themselves to the returning, demoralized men or to restore to them the position of the resolute and frequently tyrannical head of the family. Once they had learned to look after themselves, women were no longer content with the role of the wife in the kitchen, wholly given up to her family.

All that changed during the 1950s. The men recovered; an economy run by "equals," namely men, began to function and grow; and as far as relations between men and women were concerned, things returned to their prewar status. Women gradually became reconciled to their earlier, subordinate role; for many, it was plainly a relief to return to dependency after so many strenuous years. During this period, society was flooded by a wave of conservativism and a resulting regressive consolidation of families and gender relationships.

With the advent of the so-called revolution of the pill in the 1960s, the birth rate slowly began to decline from the baby-boom levels of the 1950s. The mother role lost the prestige that it had enjoyed during the conservative 1950s, when women drew from it their sense of self-esteem. During those years, a childless woman was not a "real" woman.

But how can one explain in psychological terms the renewal of the women's movement, a renewal that did not occur until during and after the student protests toward the end of the 1960s? Its initiators were women, most of whom had been born during the 1940s and thus had often retained the model of a thoroughly independent mother, one who could and had to hold her own both inside and outside of the family. Their fathers, on the other hand, were either absent or had returned more or less broken from the war.

This generation of women, many of whom took part in the student movement during the late 1960s, had for the most part adjusted—like their mothers—to the restoration of the family during the 1950s. Perhaps one may assume, however, that a longing for the independent and decisive mother of the early childhood years remained unconsciously intact and was intensified by the insecurity of a relationship with a long-absent father whose sense of self-worth had been destroyed. These women's later involvement in the women's movement was the result not only of identification with a virtuous mother but also of a desire to become inwardly less dependent on her. By developing a capacity for solidarity with other women, they heightened this wish. For the exaggerated dependence on a mother who had raised the family alone had also unleashed underlying feelings of hate, which, in turn, produced guilt feelings and depression.

In the late 1960s, many female students at first identified with their male colleagues, for whom obedience and conformity were no longer the highest rule of conduct, and adopted their antiauthoritarian stance. At the same time, they still suffered from the effects of their comrades' double standard, which demanded the same submission to them that it always had. So in the student movement, too (in fact, particularly there), women became increasingly aware of patriarchal relations of dominance and came to recognize their sadomasochistic foundations, that is, many men's pleasure in oppressing and the willingness of far too many women to be oppressed.

Domination can only be maintained when it is based on concealed sadomasochistic gratification. In such cases, one person's pleasure in issuing orders is combined with another's pleasure in discharging them and enjoyment of obedience, order, and submission. Of course, human relationships of this type exist not only between men and women but also between members of the same sex, that is, in relationships that produce not merely pleasure but also intense underlying aggression. In the absence of such a sadomasochistic social structure, it would be difficult to conduct wars. One can serve only one master, as the saying goes. By becoming aware of this ideology of obedience and questioning it, one can learn to think critically, to weigh various demands, ideals, and concepts of value against one another; in so doing, at least *one* prerequisite for freeing oneself from the necessity of blind submission will have been fulfilled.

After the student movement all but collapsed and the men of that generation had largely accustomed themselves to the ruling social order, the women's movement was able to maintain itself as a socially important process, despite its many internal and external problems.

This may be recognized in the efforts of even conservative politicians in Germany to foster amicable relations with the women's movement. What they understand by women's liberation may be gleaned from brochures with titles like "The Gentle Power of the Family." Although this group's idea of healing earthly miseries by means of worldwide motherhood may appear touching, the reality and double standard of our conservative politicians who feel free to prescribe how one ought to live is simply outrageous. This fantasy of a combination of the "sacred family" and world salvation can only be regarded as unadulterated hypocrisy.

In truth it is the powerful who rule the earth. This

includes the power of men over women and the parents over their children. Accordingly, those who dominate define what constitutes violence, but in order to obfuscate the issue, the concept of violence is employed in a paradoxical manner. Those who demonstrate against the installation of missiles by blocking traffic, for example, are violent; those who install the rockets and thereby make possible the death of countless people are considered nonviolent. When it suits the powerful, pacifism itself can become a form of violence, making possible the Second World War and even Auschwitz. The Minister of the Family in West Germany used the word *violence* when attacking reformation of the abortion laws. Those in power can also stipulate whose job it is to be maternal and gentle and when; who can bring children into the world and when; what roles women are to accept without protest; when they are to participate in devastating wars; when they are to consolidate the "gentle power of the family" and sacrifice themselves to that end, and so on.

Recently I was asked why so many women are afraid of power and whether this had anything to do with women being more afraid of losing the approval of others than of being oppressed. The question already contained its own answer: Any woman who possesses power must reckon with loss of love. Such women are often destined to be hated, not only by men but also by other women who feel powerless. I think that we are all familiar with the rage that one feels—either as a working woman, as a partner, or as a mother—when one is expected to be responsible for anything and everything while lacking the power to change things; or when one—out of fear of rejection— does not desire that power. As women, we are as inclined as ever to convert our underlying aggression into self-reproach and self-sacrifice and thus practice a form of passive aggression that is unsatisfactory to both ourselves and those whom it affects.

A woman who decides to use her capabilities freely, to arrive at her own decisions independently, to struggle for a change in her own conduct and that of others, and to overcome her fear of inevitable aggression—such a woman must relinquish her masochistic notions of innocence and self-reproach. This is not an easy task, but without such women's critical (and self-critical) revolt, nothing in this society will change. This also presupposes that women will learn to become more conscious of their aggression and to bear their guilt feelings more adequately. Women may want to change the relations between the sexes, but they will never do so without aggression and pain. Conflicts are inescapable—with loved ones, on the job, and, above all, with partners and in the family. They are unavoidable and will have to be worked through.

A further problem relating to how women's aggression is managed might be placed under the rubric "mothers and power." In the women's movement, there has been much talk about hatred of the mother: Mothers are said to hinder their daughters' development toward independence. Daughters are said to be unable to separate themselves from their mothers because the latter do not permit them to outgrow their infantile dependence without suffering guilt feelings and separation anxieties. Mothers prohibit their daughters from exercising control over their own bodies, over their sexuality. "The legacy of mothers is capitulation," according to Phyllis Chesler.

In order to preserve existing power relationships, various subterfuges are constantly being employed, not only in politics but in psychology. From all sides, women are persuaded that they are the ones who possess all of the power in the family. Only by exercising this power gently, it is said, will they be able to change the evil ways of this world. Women too easily allow themselves to be influenced by such hackneyed distortions of reality and then protest that they don't want power anyway.

Consequently, it is difficult for many women to handle power. They studiously avoid positions of authority and influence. It would appear as though they were mistaking psychoanalytic notions of the omnipotence of the mother, which are intended to apply to the experience of a small child, for social reality. Childhood fantasies and reality are equated, and social reality perceived only in a distorted form. As a result, many analytically trained women suppress their desire for independence and convert their aggression into a form of self-sacrificing masochism, even though they know better. By blaming their mothers, women once again deluge themselves with guilt, retreating into the role of a dependent servant.

But if women's power and capacity for success are not only under assault from men but are being hindered by the disparagement of members of their own sex, it will be difficult to change existing power and gender relationships. The fact is that a woman who attempts to gain influence in order to overcome established social structures may encounter scorn even from other women. She may be said to identify herself with male forms of conduct and to be doing the women's movement no service. Thus women may be forced by their own kind to suppress their abilities and potential and to act out their aggression exclusively among themselves. Under such conditions, no new ideas arise, modes of behavior cannot be changed, and all forms of creativity are lost. Against this, too, a woman must defend herself.

The "new motherhood" fantasy of salvation and overharmonizing conflict-avoiding behavior promoted in some sectors of the women's movement is an example of the new dangers that lie in store for us. Communal life without conflict and aggression would be a pseudoparadise in which, even if it were possible, one would probably die of boredom. Furthermore, much of what women have thus far achieved is slated to be undermined by new political trends. In the meantime, women must even fight attempts to repeal proabortion laws, though many no longer feel up to the task. The retreat by some women into romantic nostalgia, mystical ideas, religious sects, or astrology might be explained from a psychoanalytic point of view by the fact that the present generation of young women identified itself in early childhood not with the mothers of the wartime and postwar years, who had learned to live an independent life, but with the mothers of the 1950s who readapted themselves to earlier passive, subordinate roles and had supported the regressive, unenlightened consolidation of family and gender relationships.

In the context of psychoanalytic attempts at explanation, it seems appropriate to return to the formation of the masculine and feminine superego, its relation to the development of drives, and, in particular, to the role of aggression in shaping a person's conscience. According to Freud, the superego represents an internalization of paternal authority, an internalization accomplished fully only by men, owing to their castration anxiety. By means of this internalization of paternal prohibitions, a man inhibits his murderous aggression toward his father by directing it against his own ego. That is, he suffers from guilt and the unconscious need to punish himself. In order to escape this painful pressure, he is inclined to look for scapegoats, which enable him to displace his own repressed, anxiety-producing aggression outward and project it onto others. Our culture allows, and even demands, greater aggression in men, who are also encouraged more strongly than women to act them out. At the same time, due to his castration anxiety, a man must suppress this aggression more vigorously, internalizing it in order not to harm himself. Thus he is forced to redirect his aggression outward, and his socially formed conscience, in turn, contributes to the aggressiveness of society. It is a vicious circle, one that cannot be easily broken.

In his essay "Civilization and Its Discontents" ([1930] 1963) Freud focused his psychoanalytic interpretation primarily on the development of the male superego in relation to larger trends in society. There is little mention of how women manage their aggressive drives, for, according to Freud, the superego, which in men is so bound up with aggression and castration anxiety, is only partially developed in women. In consequence, women are also less susceptible to men's tendency and need to project onto others those anxiety-producing feelings that they abhor in themselves; men do this in order to defend themselves against self-destructive tendencies and persecute the victims of their irrational aggressions without suffering guilt.

But if one holds to this theory, the internalization of parental prohibitions by girls, which comes about more from fear of loss of love than from castration anxiety, can lead not only to a "weak superego" but also to the formation of a superego more oriented toward preserving the love of close ones than to the dutiful observance of prohibitions and commandments for their own sake. Feminine "morality" might therefore be more loving and humane than the rigid affect-isolating one of the male world, both theoretically and in practice. Due to their orientation toward objects and their pressing need to be loved, women are subject to the danger, however, of identifying with male laws, notions of value, rules of conduct, and prejudices.

Since it would seem that women remain more dependent than men on their relationships with others, and thus attempt to suppress their aggression toward them, they are more easily manipulated, particularly through guilt. Such manipulation always has something to do with the early mother-daughter relationship as well, for the conflicts triggered by Oedipal ambivalence and its predecessors are particularly intense owing to the complete dependency that characterizes early childhood.

The psychoanalyst Melanie Klein saw in women's greater dependence on their fellow human objects the result of a particularly early completion of superego formation; that is, the woman introjects her aggression with respect to a disappointing mother in the very first years of life. This internalized aggression (or "bad internalizations," as Klein called it) unleashes intense feelings of guilt and paranoic anxiety. In order to escape from these guilt feelings, a girl is more in need of external objects that provide her with love than a boy is. Klein traced gender-specific distinctions in superego formation to the physical givens of men and women. A boy has an advantage with respect to a girl in that his sex, a visible and graspable organ, one verifiable by reality-testing, enables him to feel independent of the mother more easily. He is a different sort of being, in possession of something that she lacks. Yet such interpretations, though certainly interesting, largely ignore childrearing and cultural influences on the parents' conduct and on a child's development. Doubtless it is important to recognize and classify early childhood factors in order to better understand the complex process of superego formation in women, as well as in men. But if we overlook the role of economic and social circumstances and their effects on childrearing, we run the risk of regarding a person's psychic development and a child's relationship to its parents as if they were taking place in a vacuum.

I will attempt, using a female patient as an example, to make several issues related to the formation of aggression and the superego somewhat clearer.

A young woman, Sara, sought treatment for episodes of depression, a tendency to self-hatred, and social anxieties. She was married but had largely separated from her husband, though they remained on friendly terms. The cause of their separation was a man of Eastern European extraction, several years her senior, with whom she had fallen in love. He was extraordinarily important to her, and she felt herself drawn to him particularly because of his foreign background. She also claimed that until then she had never been able to be so open about her feelings with anyone.

The feelings that this man aroused in her, however, were remarkably ambivalent. She felt herself to be completely understood yet, at the same time, utterly ignored. It was a difficult relationship, one that had profoundly shaken her, but at the same time a close and loving one.

When this man returned to his own country, where a family awaited him, she became deeply depressed. Never again, she told herself, would she be able to become emotionally involved with another person. Her confusion was genuine, and over a period of time, her distress had reached the limits of the tolerable. She was capable, intelligent, able to learn, and gave those around her the impression of being competent, even cool.

Sara's childhood had been a difficult one. When she was about six years old, her parents separated, and her father scorned her mother as a sexually licentious, poorly educated woman. Her mother was afraid of her father, whose intellectual acuity and mercilessness sometimes hurt her and her daughters. Both apparently overlooked the father's neurotic misery and loneliness; they idealized him despite, or perhaps because of, the wrongs he did them. Ultimately, both parents remarried; the patient remained with her mother, whom Sara thought had accommodated herself too thoroughly to circumstances in the stepfather's house. The atmosphere there was largely determined by the moral and social orientation of the stepfather's family.

Like her mother, Sara was overly dependent on being loved and thus adjusted herself to suit the demands of her environment more than was good for her. She often felt overtaxed and thought that she could rarely be open and assert her own needs.

In addition to her mother's readiness to conform to the values of her environment, Sara had also internalized much of the intellectual and moral cruelty of her father's conduct. Just as she had never felt that her father recognized her own mental capabilities, so she was never able to achieve a more or less stable, loving regard for either her mother or herself. Despite all her abilities, she was insecure and anxious, but also very aggressive. She was at the same time severe and far too compliant toward other people.

With respect to the social side of her superego, Sara was active in the women's movement, and her political interests were marked by a strong moral impetus. She had quite obviously been looking, in her friend, for a portion of a lost relationship with her mother; she drank in the warmth and intensity of his feelings for her like a person dying of thirst. She even made his values into her own, though they were influenced by another culture and in their own way were as hard, severe, and intransigent as her father's, especially with regard to politics. Her superego was divided; to the extent that it bore her mother's stamp, it seemed all too obliging, requiring love, and inducing guilt, social anxiety, self-denigration, and the resultant depressions. To the extent that she had internalized her father's attitudes, on the other hand, Sara's superego was hard and judgmental and also highly self-critical, reflecting her father's own fears of inadequacy.

Later in life, the man with whom she was so in love combined the two parental superego authorities as she had experienced them in her early and later childhood. The separation from him was particularly painful because it represented a repetition of a childhood trauma, intensifying her inclination to self-hatred. We discussed her self-destructive tendencies during her analysis.

Sara's relationships took on such a difficult form because her animosity and deprecating tendencies often vented themselves not only on herself but on others. When she became aware of this, her conduct changed drastically; she became masochistically apologetic, characterized herself as a failure, and tended to make amends for her aggression by reproaching herself. The resultant sadomasochistic vi-

cious circle and underlying aggression associated with it
on the one hand, and the guilt and fear of loss of love on
the other, interfered with the development of a lasting
adult relationship, that is with her capacity to manage her
own feelings of ambivalence and guilt consciously.

I would like to return now to the different ways in which
the two sexes deal with their feelings of guilt. Men, as
numerous observations confirm, are more strongly inclined to deny and repress their guilt feelings than are
women, who are often condemned to suffer them help-
lessly. They would be well advised indeed to deal with
their receptiveness to guilt feelings more critically, for
there is nothing that can be exploited more easily than
such feelings. But in so doing, one must not overlook the
important role that unconscious guilt feelings play in the
mental life of all individuals, nor the tenacious defense
mechanisms that are erected to prevent these feelings, for
which aggression is often the source, from becoming conscious.

The deep-rooted fear of destroying the love of those
closest to one through one's own aggression and deni-
grating attitudes is often particularly insurmountable for
women. As a result of their exaggerated need for love,
they often react in a depressive manner to their unconscious guilt; this only aggravates their tendency to be dependent on the opinions and approval of others. In turn,
exaggerated feelings of guilt awaken underlying aggression that, in turn, calls forth more guilt. Men who repress
their aggression out of castration anxiety, that is, from
fear of reprisals and physical abuse rather than from fear
of loss of love, suffer depressions less frequently than do

women, for what they fear is not the loss of a love object but their own physical destruction.

Guilt and the self-hatred associated with it are thus less important in men or are repressed more successfully. Men protect themselves against their anxiety-producing internalized aggression primarily by projecting it onto others, that is, they find scapegoats and rivals onto whom they can project their aggression and fantasies of revenge without guilt or anxiety, thus acting them out where possible.

Women's passive-aggressive and dependent conduct and their willingness to suffer are encouraged by gender-specific socialization, which has always allowed men to be aggressive, self-assertive, and to repress emotions, while allocating an accommodating, emotional, and subservient role to women. But men, too, react with animosity to their dependence on women, and the withdrawal of maternal care often provokes in them helpless anxiety and rage.

But how can we deal better with an entrenched system of psychic and social gender relationships? There is both little and much we can do here. With rigid, centuries-old mechanisms of conduct—no matter how they may appear to have changed in some respects, at least to the superficial observer—a fundamental revision will obviously be difficult to accomplish. If those in the women's movement act out their intense aggression among themselves, instead of rethinking it and directing it into suitable channels, they run the risk of throwing away their only chance of influencing the structure of existing society. They will then have only confirmed those psychoanalytic theories that hold that women, as a result of an unresolved negative bonding to the mother, are more inclined than men to act out their aggressive feelings among members of their own sex. Instead, women must make their aggression conscious or develop a new self-image in order to break out of the role expectations to which they are subject. Emotional ties to the mother change during the course of a lifetime, but identification with her forms of behavior and with her unresolved conflicts, indeed with her fantasies and false notions of happiness, have a tendency to repeat themselves.

Moreover, women run the risk of experiencing themselves as an appendage to a career-bound husband, thus solidifying his repression of emotions and his fantasies of power and omnipotence which are often coupled with fears of persecution and the search for scapegoats. Such women remain chained to stereotypical forms of behavior—the self-sacrificing housewife, for example, who shares her husband's mask of ambition as well as his paranoid inclinations and search for rivals. In men these tendencies have, among other things, found expression in the widespread mentality of the arms race.

The more critically women reexamine their social roles and psychic reactions for their meaning and underlying content, the more false guilt and identifications will be undermined and questioned for their legitimacy. Despite the pessimism about regressive and reactionary tendencies, this change may also be increasingly seen in the women's movement. Not a few women are spurning the rules of the game and the role expectations of our social structure, which remains as patriarchal as in the past. One may also observe a perceptible awakening to the psychic and cultural situation in which everyone has to live, as well as a more anxiety-free manner of managing aggression in all kinds of situations. The extent to which a woman is capable of doing this depends in turn largely upon whether she succeeds in making conscious unconscious motives that lie at the root of both her own behavior and that of society as a whole.

2

Aggression and Gender

ARE THERE such things as male and female forms of aggression, or even male and female death drives? Most women and men—colleagues and noncolleagues—whom I have asked about gender-specific forms of aggression have replied in the affirmative. They found it harder to describe in greater detail what they regarded as typical female and male forms of aggression.

A psychoanalyst might well answer more or less as follows: "Yes, there is a difference between male and female forms of aggression. Women's aggressions, insofar as they are related to anal and phallic strivings, tend to be turned inward, are more masochistic than sadistic, and less direct. Their superegos are 'weaker' and more easily influenced but also inclined toward projection. Their sense of self is more easily undermined by envy than that of men; jealousy plays an important role, but it is less bound up with aggressions of rivalry than in men and more hidden, and women resort to reproach more frequently.

"The 'weak' superego of women predestines them to sublimate their drives less effectively, to achieve less in science and art. Their ethics and morality are oriented toward external prohibitions, toward the rules of men and the society they dominate. But because of the emotionality of their 'weak' superegos, sudden, unrestrained outbreaks of aggression can occur in women; these might seem surprising, but they are to be expected, for women carry around a more than ample supply of guilt feelings (though repressed). How else could one explain men's underlying fear of women's emotions?"

This male fear of sudden, violent outbursts of aggression in otherwise docile women can be amply documented. Schiller, himself a revolutionary and an honorary citizen of the French Republic by as early as 1792, wrote about the wicked conduct of women during the French Revolution: "Here, women have become hyenas and make sport of horror. Still quivering, they tear apart their enemies' hearts with the teeth of panthers."

Most people still regard women who take part in revolutionary activities as perverse. There was widespread disbelief when it turned out that some European terrorist groups were made up of at least as many women as men. Women were criticized even more strongly than their male comrades for their deviant behavior and inhumanity. Most of them came from well-to-do middle-class families, a milieu in which one would expect women to conform. The women terrorists transgressed all boundaries of what had always been regarded as predictable female conduct; their misconduct engendered general incredulity and anger. Some had left their husbands and children; others eschewed heterosexual relationships.

The middle class is likewise perplexed by the fact that lesbian relationships are becoming increasingly common. The search for scapegoats begins once again. What else than the women's movement, usually scorned by the middle class anyway, could be responsible for these awful, shocking developments?

Most psychoanalysts, too, regard feminists as unnatural or ridiculous and, if possible, will have nothing to do with them. They are in the habit of labeling them "phallic women." Whatever women can muster in the way of self-assertion, envy, or even creativity is frequently designated "phallic" by psychoanalysts. This cliché is supposed to prove to women that they are living in a world of illusions; they are obviously unable to free themselves from the fantasy of having a penis.

Psychoanalytic pronouncements about femininity often become muddled in stereotypes about the "nature of women." A woman who refuses to accept her "deficiency" is defending herself against reality by wishful thinking. She has not reached, it is said, the stage of "mature femininity," the genital stage.

If one has already classified feminists according to a psychoanalytic system, taking them seriously becomes unnecessary, for their conduct, their achievements, their revolt against a society ruled by men, is, of course, based on a fantasy. Only the actual possession of a phallus would legitimize such conduct, only then would it be "natural" for a woman to rebel against the injustice she encounters daily. According to this view, women are realistic only when they direct their aggressiveness and belligerence inward, make the family the locus of their activities, and sacrifice themselves to their husband and children, or when they sublimate their cravings for love in service professions.

In numerous books, women have attempted to show

that Freud's ideas and theories stand in the way of women's efforts to achieve emancipation and equality. It is true that to a large extent Freud acepted his society's notions about the role and nature of women. While doing research on the philospher and women's rights advocate John Stuart Mill, he translated an essay by Mill's lifelong companion Harriet Taylor ([1851] 1970) entitled "On the Emancipation of Women"; in a much-quoted 1893 letter to his future wife, Martha Bernays, he wrote: "Law and custom have much to give women that has been withheld from them, but the position of women will surely be what it is: in youth an adored darling and in mature years a loved wife" (Jones 1953).

But why did Freud choose to translate this particular essay, at the time still attributed to Mill but in fact written in 1851 by Harriet Taylor? It must have been a topic that stirred his interest, and it evoked a typical male reaction from him, as his letter to his wife shows. Freud apparently fell prey to a fear of independence in women and of their demands for equality. How else could one explain his letter?

In the works of August Strindberg, who was born only seven years before Freud, one can see what panic can be produced in men by the notion of a woman who does not center herself, her life, her thoughts, and her sexuality exclusively around her husband. Strindberg, who was a militant in the cause of socialism and the elimination of class discrimination, defended himself most violently, and sparing no invective, against equal rights for women and the elimination of sex discrimination. Of course, Strindberg was a very unstable, overly sensitive man, and susceptible to paranoic breakdowns. But often it is just such hypersensitive people who reveal most clearly what is going on in the psyches of their contemporaries.

During the 1920s and through the mid-1930s, the psychosexual development of women was the subject of numerous debates within the psychoanaytic community. But thereafter the discussion subsided almost entirely, and the views of analysts who disagreed with Freud largely disappeared. In 1964, however, a volume of essays on female sexuality by J. Chasseguet-Smirgel was published in Paris. Most of the authors of this volume appeared to be aligned with the English school of Melanie Klein. Starting about 1970, other psychoanalysts also began slowly to concern themselves with the psychosexual development of women. In 1976, Harold Blum published a collection of psychoanalytic papers on the psychology of women in the *Journal of the American Psychoanalytic Association*. In 1975 and 1978, two volumes of the journal *Psyche* were devoted to the theme of femininity.

But one cannot avoid the impression that these discussions have been generally ignored by male and female psychoanalysts alike. They continue to talk complacently of penis envy, phallic women, true femininity, infantile wishes as a substitute for a penis, and so forth. Many analysts seem to regard Freud's hypotheses about female sexuality as a proven theory. This attitude may be regarded as a form of defense. Those in power do not like to question themselves. In theory, psychoanalysts may well know that something approaching reality can only become apparent through constantly renewed efforts to critically examine one's own conduct and theories, and that one can liberate oneself from thought prohibitions and compulsions only by making unconscious motives conscious. But in practice, this knowledge does not prevent them from clinging to theories that they are comfortable with and that spare them from having to revise their attitudes.

Christa Rohde-Dachser ("Women as Psychotherapists; The Janus Face of Emancipation and Its Consequences," ca. 1982) has examined the problems of being both a woman and a psychoanalyst, a position that involves a particular type of role conflict. As a therapist, a woman is conforming to a standard role by developing tact, a capacity for empathy, calm, patience, and the ability to be receptive to others while simultaneously having access to her own feelings. These characteristics are also expected of male therapists, although in our society, male therapists tend to be regarded as feminine. Thus both men and women appear to cultivate and act out their "femininity" in psychoanalytic therapy. But this acting out is only possible to an extent, because women psychoanalysts are expected to be sexually neutral. In all other areas of the psychoanalytic profession, on the other hand, in professional organizations and research projects, for example, modes of behavior that are much more typical of male role stereotypes are demanded. In these areas, as one might expect, few women are to be found. Moreover, the role conflict of women psychoanalysts is aggravated by the internalization of a largely negative women-and-motherhood stereotype that they have learned and internalized during the course of their psychoanalytic socialization.

But Rohde-Dachser has made another point: "The social conflict to which women (and working women in particular) are subject is usually regarded by psychoanalysts as an intrapsychic conflict, in accordance with their psychoanalytic training. Complaints about social injustice are considered embarrassing because they represent a confession of their own shortcomings. The theory that women deny objective realities and compensate with fantasies of omnipotence has turned out to be above question."

Issues of the *International Journal of Psychoanalysis* or *Imago* from the 1930s astound one with the liveliness and clinical immediacy of the discussion surrounding issues related specifically to women. In the volumes for 1933–1934 alone, there were some fourteen articles concerned with the psychosexual development of women or with phallic defensive mechanisms in men. Lilian Rotter (1934) attempted to explain male fears of women and of their sexual power over men; they provoke erections beyond a man's control, often through their mere visible presence. Even a little girl, Rotter said, is aware of her sexual power over men and builds her sense of self around being able to seduce men. When during sexual childplay a little girl discovers that she can cause erections, it awakens the feeling in her that the penis is subject to her control and is thus also a part of her own body. Thus penis envy would only appear, according to Rotter, when a woman has the feeling that her influence over men has disappeared. In accordance with this female experience, some men regard woman as the "true owner of the penis." Rotter's paper does not take into account what it means for both the man and the woman when the man is incapable of having an erection, and the woman thus cannot "manipulate" him. The hatred that this triggers in both, which is perhaps not merely the consequence but also the source of the man's impotence, should not be underestimated. Freud established early on that the frustration of sexual desires can call forth considerable aggression in both sexes. The basis of homosexuality is occasionally that a man, instead of a woman, has the power to excite other men or confront them with their impotence. But if a woman's sense of self-esteem depends on her ability to seduce men, this does not exactly promote her autonomy and creativity.

A phenomenon that one might call a Pygmalion complex can be observed in men who attempt to actualize their unconscious feminine identification and secret infantile wishes, while at the same time needing confirmation of their power over women. They occupy themselves intensively with young women, by cultivating their students or patients, for example; they breathe new life into them by imparting their experience and their knowledge, making them into quasi-newborn creatures, or ones capable of orgasm for the first time.

An interesting example of the Pygmalion complex was the relationship between Jean-Paul Sartre and Simone de Beauvoir. De Beauvoir refused to have children and became wholly involved with Sartre, who was of the opinion that the only thing that counted in the life of men and women was their works. Sartre had been able to convince even his first fiancée, Camille, of this view, and thus had also succeeded in bringing that self-assured, independent, and ambitious woman under his spell. In producing creations of the mind, according to Sartre, man and woman are united on a plane of fertility. Sartre, who surely identified himself to a large extent with women, preferred their company to that of men. His sexuality was marked by a need for tenderness; his genital potency was apparently not particularly pronounced, and was, it seems, of no great significance to him. Despite, or perhaps exactly because of this, he succeeded in making himself the center of interest of a number of women, many of whom surrounded him to the very end of his life.

Freud ([1905] 1963) recognized that the first great problem with which a child concerns itself is not the question of the difference between the sexes but that of where children come from. Not until a boy discovers that he is incapable of bearing children does he begin to attach particular importance to being different from his mother, a task in which he is supported by society. This suggests that the discovery of penis envy itself might be an expression of male wishes to make women as jealous of anatomy, and the abilities that go along with it, as men are of women. Perhaps Freud had to emphasize over and over again that jealousy and envy are primarily female characteristics in order to repress his own feelings of jealousy and envy.

3

Man-hating and Woman-hating

FEMINISTS ARE frequently accused of being man-haters. Alice Schwarzer (1977) noted that for her, the women's movement was a struggle for women and their emancipation, not a campaign against men. Only when men try to hinder women's struggle for emancipation would she fight against them, she wrote: "Whoever wants to do away with hatred must eliminate its sources."

There is ample occasion for hatred. We need only look around us, and everywhere we encounter people who condemn others to misery, torture, murder, or starvation. We Germans need only think of our recent past. There is no shortage of past and present situations in which women have had to delimit themselves to suit men and their notions of behavior. Moreover, it is above all women who have been debased, scorned, and exploited for hundreds of years in our patriarchally structured society. For many centuries, woman-hating by men was the rule, and hardly anyone spoke of man-hating by women. In numerous manifestoes, novels, and supposedly scholarly dissertations, famous men of the past and present have held forth on the character flaws of women and their feeble-mindedness, and have questioned whether they could even be considered people at all. Throughout history men have preached hatred and contempt for women.

Ever since women have attempted to break free of the contempt and self-contempt into which male attitudes have forced them, and have begun to fight together for their rights, they have been accused of being man-haters. Is the man-hating for which many of our contemporaries reproach women itself a displacement of a mother-hating that has its origins in early childhood? Those who have studied the emotional development of women at length know that women's early relations with the mother are extremely varied, and that later relations with men, as well as with women, can develop in fundamentally differing ways. Severe traumas in early childhood and early disruptions of the mother-child relationship can gravely affect a woman's later life. The following is provided by way of example:

> A female patient came from a working-class family. The father, an uneducated laborer, showed no interest in the family after separating from the mother. The mother, a waitress, had habitually left the patient, who was an only child, alone in the evenings. At night she often returned home intoxicated and accompanied by a lover. Maria, as I shall call my patient, experienced the couple's loud conduct during sexual intercourse as something strange and disruptive. She was a deeply anxious child, one who tried to act out her abandonment in school by being rebellious and sometimes gained popularity with her classmates in this way.

Those in her social environment made quite clear to her how greatly her mother was scorned for her disreputable life-style. After leaving school, she became a waitress like her mother, then a barmaid; like her mother, she had numerous sexual relationships with men and began to drink. She finally married a man who was something of a playboy and could offer her a life free from material concerns. Their happiness lasted only a short while, however, since no deeper relationship developed between the two partners. Maria felt disappointed and occasionally fell prey to anxiety attacks, whose cause eluded her. Every few weeks she would disappear for several days, during which time she was usually constantly intoxicated. While on her alcoholic binges, she had numerous sexual encounters. Usually these involved contact with married couples, with whom she would lie in bed at night. Her longing for a loving married couple to satisfy her childlike wishes for protection was clearly apparent in this conduct.

But the real motive for her flight was her feeling of being persecuted, a feeling that rationally she regarded as senseless but that she could only hold in check with the help of alcohol. She found support in a group of former alcoholics who were attempting to help each other. Such people behave toward each other in the way that siblings who have lost their mother often do.

In this patient, who had suffered unusual traumas in her childhood, the sexual triangles represented an attempt to convince herself that her parents loved her, and thus concealed her helpless rage at her parents and her social environment. This rage was the source of her feelings of persecution and caused her to fear revenge and irrevocable abandonment. Basically the patient suffered from the consequences of early-childhood neglect, of a deficit in maternal and parental relationships, as René Spitz has characterized it. Thus, for the patient, it was preferable to identify herself with her alcoholic mother, after whom her conduct was ultimately modeled, than to fear and hate her mother and feel herself persecuted or completely abandoned by her.

Another fragment from an analysis should make clear the predestining effect of an underlying animosity toward the mother.

A young patient, Clara, who had had a strict Catholic upbringing repeatedly fell in love with Catholic priests. Not surprisingly, each of these relationships ended in disappointment. One might easily have assumed that this was a case of Oedipal situations being repeated, that is, that the priest represented a father with whom the patient had entertained incestuous relations for which she was compelled to punish herself.

As the therapy proceeded, it became evident that Clara was strongly dependent on her mother, however, and it increasingly appeared that the priests with whom she had established her relationships were, in fact, disguised mother figures. Clara longed above all for a mother who could treat her with understanding. But she had suffered a disappointment at an early age: Her mother, whom she so admired and loved, preferred her brother and showed little empathy and understanding for the emotional life of her daughter. The ambivalence, even hatred, that was evoked in her by this unjust, incomprehensible, but probably typical apportioning of love was naturally the source of considerable anxiety. Thus, in order to gratify her need for love she later displaced her desires to priests, pseudofathers who also displayed clear maternal traits.

Since in her family, sexual matters were repressed with

particular severity, and masturbation was regarded as a sin, Clara developed intense feelings of guilt and inferiority as well, for despite her tormented efforts she was unable to give up masturbating. This in turn intensified her underlying feelings of hatred.

In addition to her unhappy love affairs, Clara suffered from a mild dependency on sleeping pills, taking harmless drugs that could scarcely have had any effect on her sleep but without which she nevertheless could not fall asleep. Not until her hatred toward her mother was brought to light, and it became possible to convey a feeling of dependable empathy to her during the course of the therapy, did Clara's sense of self improve sufficiently for her to risk and succeed in falling asleep without her sleeping pills.

The way in which many young women attempt to sexually "incorporate" or consume their idealized male friends is reminiscent of early-childhood oral forms of initiating relationships. Female patients suffering from the trauma of an early-childhood disruption of the mother-child relationship, and whose fathers did share in raising the children, often display drug abuse or alcoholism in addition to their addictive sexual behavior, as in the case of the aforementioned patient.

Edward Shorter (1975) noted, drawing on Marx, that present social and cultural norms are heavily influenced by the egoism conditioned by the marketplace. Human relations thus become determined by a barter mentality; everyone wants to acquire his or her "merchandise" as cheaply as possible. The relationship between mother and child is a different type of interaction, for it lacks the egoistic give and take (and hence the egoism) that is bent on its own advantage, or at least on making sure in a petty sort of way that give and take are appropriately balanced. The mother-child relationship is dominated by forms of feeling and relating that are fundamentally distinct from the ethics of the marketplace. Perhaps it is for this reason as well that our society overidealizes mothers on the one hand but vehemently condemns women on the other. One might well ask whether unconscious identification with *male* woman-hating is concealed behind "mother-hating" in women.

In more searching discussions with men, one is often surprised to hear that fundamentally they do not look up to members of their own sex but prefer relationships with women, including simply friendships. But the majority have become set in their ways in marriage and career and show hardly any signs of change. Out of fear of being unmanly, many men deny and repress their dependent needs and withdraw from discussion at home as an emotional defense, or believe that they have to be unfaithful to their wives to prove their manhood, thus covering up for their dependency and perhaps transferring it onto another woman.

The withdrawn man who wants to be both spoiled and admired is (to the extent that he is an "intellectual") primarily concerned with finding himself; he should be examined closely for the sources of his stereotypical conduct and his unconscious fantasies of greatness. Such men often idealize themselves as loners. They believe that they must conceal their feelings in order to be able to satisfactorily keep up the masculine role they have adopted.

Fantasies of greatness associated with sex-role stereotypes play less of a role in women than in men. But women are subject to the danger of experiencing themselves as a part of the career-conscious husband, thus sharing in his fantasies of greatness. In such cases, women too become tied to sex-role stereotypes, such as that of the self-sacrificing housewife who devotes herself wholly to promoting her husband's success. The more a woman identifies with her husband and integrates herself into existing power hierarchies, the harder it will be for her to become conscious of prevailing values and ideals and to free herself from them. But such women, too, eventually become aware of how little their self-sacrificing role does for them, and they react with underlying jealousy and hatred, which, in turn, is often repressed with renewed masochistic behavior.

M. Torok (1964) saw penis envy as merely a defense against an original hatred toward the mother, who a little girl feels controls her anal functions and interferes with her masturbatory wishes, thus prohibiting her from enjoying her own sexuality. Her hatred toward the mother, whom she also loves and depends on more than any other person during her childhood, produces intense guilt. Though she identifies to a large extent with a mother she experiences as power hungry, a girl remains fixated to a sadomasochistic phase of development as a result of her guilt and fails to grow out of this phase. Behind penis envy lies the wish to work through unsolved conflicts with the mother; such conflicts stand in the way of maturation, self-definition, and the resolution of internal conflicts. If a girl's dependence on the mother is not broken, the usual result is a similar dependency on a husband or partner. Such dependencies are, in general, encouraged by the world of men. For a man, too, fears the mother of the anal phase, experienced as a danger, and attempts to protect himself against this dependency by identifying with a phallic father. Anxiety, dependency, guilt, and animosity toward the mother remain in place and are projected onto the wife, whose lack of independence the man experiences as a relief, as something that alleviates his anxiety and animosity.

Men's original feelings of jealousy and animosity toward the mother have often been noted, and much has been written about their envy of giving birth and having breasts. For a man, displacing his envy onto a woman means experiencing his own envy and dependency consciously. Thus he seeks all kinds of justifications for his feelings of anxiety, rage, and aggression toward women (which in fact stem from early childhood), depending on whatever the norms of his era happen to be. He brands them as witches, stupid, or as particularly narcissistic. Hate-filled pejoratives associated with women are legion.

Disappointment with the mother and unresolved conflict associated with her, which can give rise to intense hatred, are in my opinion often wrongly assigned to the symbiotic or oral stages. Their roots often lie in the anal phase. Put more precisely: Since it is not exclusively a question of the development of a drive, but also of relational conflicts, the disruption of the mother-child relationship usually does not occur until the phase of separation and individuation, during which there is ample opportunity for conflicting urges to develop. As later, during puberty, it is difficult for many mothers to come to terms with their daughters' normal age-related desires for separation in this period. Puberty is frequently characterized by especially intense mother-daughter conflicts; in such cases mothers are seeking a substitute for their own marital disappointments in the continuation of a close relationship with their daughters into adulthood, perhaps unconsciously repeating their own mothers' behavior toward them.

4

The Socialization of Women

THE TERM *socialization* applies to the sum total of the phases a person passes through during the course of development, the "sociocultural birth" by means of which he or she is incorporated into the social structure and network of interaction. The individual is subjected to primary socialization within the family; in the process of secondary socialization, a person is constantly learning new role behavior as well. Although the term *socialization* is not itself part of the specifically psychoanalytic vocabulary, I have used it because it strikes me as an apt expression for a person's "second," or sociocultural, birth, and thus also for the manner in which girls in a given society are made into women. To a large extent, a particular society's scheme of values determines forms of gender-specific child rearing, as well as the unconscious attitude of the parents toward their children.

The concept of "psychic birth" was first introduced to psychoanalysis by Margaret Mahler, who used it to describe the developmental period during which a child slowly breaks forth from the autistic and symbiotic phase of unity with the mother. It is at this point that the processes of individuation and separation from the mother begin. Even as early as this developmental period, it is more difficult for many mothers to come to terms with their daughters' normal age-related desire for separation than with their sons'. Thus at this stage, socialization is already occurring; traditional role guidelines increasingly influence the behavior of parents toward their children. This in turn shapes the way in which the child handles its drives and, hence, the vicissitudes of those drives.

But what do psychoanalysts mean by drives and their vicissitudes? In a paper Freud completed in April 1915, entitled "Instincts and Their Vicissitudes" ([1915a] 1963), he defined a *drive* as "a concept on the frontier of the mental and the somatic, the psychical representation of impulses originating from within the organism and reaching the mind." In another paper entitled "Repression," completed that same year, he described the psychic manifestation of a drive as an idea or group of ideas invested with a given level of psychic energy, also known as libido. For Freud, the *drive* was always a term spanning the boundaries of the mental and the somatic. In *Beyond the Pleasure Principle* ([1920] 1963) he called drives "the most important and most obscure areas of psychological research." Freud distinguished between drives and stimuli; stimuli come from the outside, drives from within. One may avoid an external impulse by flight, but instinctual demands cannot be evaded; this holds true even if drives are construed as nothing more than endogenous stimuli. Between the years 1897 and 1911, the discovery of the Oedipus complex and with it the importance of fantasy in psychological conflict were the focal points of psychoanalytic interest. Thus, during this phase in the development of Freud's theory, less attention was paid to the influence of external events and traumas than previously.

According to Freud's theory of drives, the sexual drives and the drives associated with self-preservation—known as the ego drives—find themselves in conflict with one another. The ego drives are of a repressive nature, while the sexual drives represent a force that has been repressed and strives toward consciousness and gratification. This conflict is analogous to the one between conscious and unconscious forces; the ego is still regarded as a *conscious* authority.

This was the state of psychoanalytic theory when Freud discovered and defined the *unconscious* portion of the ego. With his introduction of the concept of "narcissism" in 1914, the distinction between the sexual drives and the ego drives was blurred. Freud came to recognize that both of these drives are fed from a common source of libidinal energy. He now viewed the difference between the two as a matter of object choice; that is, the libido can direct itself either at an external object or at the ego itself. Freud continued to insist, however, that there were also *nonlibidinal* ego drives, which for the time being he called "interests." After 1914 his understanding of the significance of aggression began to change as well. Previously it had been understood within the context of sadism, as a component of the sexual drive, but it now came to be included among the nonlibidinal drives, as the drive for mastery.

Since Freud constantly found himself confronted with the problem of ambivalence—that is the simultaneous existence of love and hate in a relationship to another person or to the self or ego—the topic of aggression became increasingly important in his thinking. Beginning with *Beyond the Pleasure Principle* ([1920] 1963), Freud insisted on an opposition between the sexual and aggressive drives. The concept of "ego drives" was more or less abandoned; the self-preservative drive and the sexual drive came to be seen as aspects of a single life drive. Aggression was no longer included among the ego drives but instead among the death drives. In this phase in the development of Freud's theory of drives, the general categories of life and death were seen in opposition to one another.

Sexuality for Freud was not a single, unified drive; rather, he portrayed it as composed of a number of partial drives, such as the opposing pairs of exhibitionism and scopophilia, sadism and masochism, and so on. Until these partial drives are integrated in the genital phase, they seek gratification independently of one another. The partial drives that correspond to the oral, anal, and phallic stages of childhood development are closely associated with the erogenous zones after which they are named, which can be the sources of pleasurable stimulation.

I would like to return once more to the evolution of Freud's theory of drives, as formulated in his 1915 paper "Instincts and Their Vicissitudes" ([1915a] 1963). There, Freud described how "love," in the course of childhood development, evolves from a simple pleasure relationship between the ego and the object, and ultimately becomes fixated on the sexual object. Hate, by contrast, is associated less with sexual pleasure than with the ego drives. The "unpleasure" reaction appears to be the only decisive one in generating hate.

The ego hates, abhors, and pursues with intent to destroy all objects which are a source of unpleasurable feeling for it, without taking into account whether they mean a frustration of sexual satisfaction or of the satisfaction of the need for self-preservation. Indeed, it may be asserted that the true prototypes of the relation of hate are derived not from sexual life, but from the ego's struggle to preserve and maintain itself. Hate, as a relation to objects, is older than love. It derives from the narcissistic ego's primordial repudiation of the external world with its outpouring of stimuli. As an expression of the reaction of unpleasure evoked by objects, it always remains in an intimate relation with the self-preservative drives, so that the ego drives and the sexual drives can readily develop an antithesis which repeats that between hate and love. (Freud [1915a] 1963)

Analysts since Freud have developed other views concerning the predisposition to love or hate.

With Freud's introduction of a duality between the life and death drives in 1920, the pleasure principle was dethroned as the sole ruling authority in mental life. Freud's theory changed with the discovery that experiences are repeated even though they provide no gain of pleasure and could not have satisfied drives in the past. He recognized that there is a compulsion to repeat that overrides the pleasure principle; he described this repetition compulsion as having the characteristics of an instinct, much like those associated with the pleasure principle. "In what way are instinctual factors related to the compulsion to repeat?" Freud asked in *Beyond the Pleasure Principle* ([1920] 1963). "At this point we cannot escape the suspicion," he continued, "that we may have come upon the track of a universal attribute of drives and perhaps of organic life in general. . . . It seems, then, that a drive is an urge inherent in organic life to restore an earlier state of things. . . ." In the same paper, Freud compared the polarity between love and hate with that between the life and death drives and concerned himself with the workings of the death drive within the organism. In later writings (such as *Civilization and Its Discontents* [1930] 1963), he also directed his attention to the way in which the death drive is externalized and becomes manifest as destructive or aggressive tendencies. Death and life drives appear only rarely in unadulterated form and are usually blended or fused with each other. This theme is pursued further in "The Ego and the Id" (1923). There the concept of a "fusion" of drives is seen as an incontrovertible assumption. "The sadistic components of the sexual drive would be a classical example of an expedient fusion of drives; sadism which has made itself independent as a perversion would be typical of a defusion, though not of one carried to extremes."

After formulating the death drive theory in *Beyond the Pleasure Principle* ([1920] 1963) Freud introduced his so-called structural model of psychoanalysis in *The Ego and the Id* ([1923] 1963); here the psyche was divided into various mental authorities: ego, id, and superego.

According to Freud, the superego incorporates that share of childhood aggressiveness that the child—due to his love for them—cannot direct against its parents. The aggression was originally directed against the parents because they denied gratification of the child's drive-related desires. The internalized parents, along with their prohibitions and strictures, become a component part of the superego. But the severity of the superego does not depend only on the severity of the parents but instead (as Freud emphasized) on the quantity of aggressiveness directed at the parents by the child. This aggressiveness is turned inward and incorporated into the superego. The identifications and internalizations involved in superego formation are accompanied by a "de-fusion" of the drives; the destructive strivings within the mind thereby released increase the severity of the superego. Identification always means an at least partial abandonment of the object; that is, since love for the object recedes into the background, aggression and narcissism grow during the process of identification.

The form and content of the superego are dependent on how a person handles his or her drives and the objects to which they are attached, and thus are a consequence of the drive's development. The severity, weakness, rigidity, elasticity, one-sidedness, or variability of the superego depend on how the drives, particularly the aggressive drives, are managed during the course of an individual's development—on how human relationships are internalized; fantasies are worked through; and feelings of guilt are projected, introjected, or suffered passively; and much more. Everything that the psychoanalyst treats and attempts to understand belongs to the realm of the development of drives. Defensive mechanisms are built up against anxiety-producing or prohibited libidinal drives; such defensive mechanisms determine symptoms or the structure of the personality.

A regression of the libido, or a defense mechanism and with it a particular development of a drive, can lead to the liberation of previously inhibited destructive drives directed against an object. This occurs in obsessional neurosis, for example. Here the ego must defend itself against internalized anal-sadistic impulses.

In melancholia, in which the ego identifies with a lost object and the libido regresses to the level of narcissism, all of the destructive impulses contained within the superego, which were originally intended for the object, are likewise turned against the ego itself. Hence the inclination toward suicide that is often observed in cases of depression and melancholia. "When an instinctual trend undergoes repression, its libidinal elements are turned into symptoms, and its aggressive components into a sense of guilt," wrote Freud in *Civilization and Its Discontents*. The self-torment and self-accusations of the masochist or melancholic signify the satisfaction of sadistic and hate-filled inclinations. The illness serves to prevent the open expression of hostility toward the love object.

Every vicissitude of a drive has its own particular defensive character: The drive can be repressed; turned back toward the self; transformed into its opposite; or result in identifications, projections, or internalizations. In 1926 Freud hypothesized that "before the sharp distinction between ego and id, before the formation of a superego, the mental apparatus avails itself of other methods of defense than after this organizational stage has been achieved."

Just how a person satisfies or represses his or her drives is the personal destiny of every human being. With the sexual drives it is not only a matter of defenses against and management of the genital portion of the drive, but also one of the admissibility of pregenital partial drives and defenses against them. The agencies of the ego and superego to a large extent determine the development of a person's drives and the types of symptoms and character formations that arise through defense or gratification. At the same time, the formation of the superego must itself be understood as the outcome of a drive, above all as the outcome of aggression. When shame, guilt, and abhorrence have not yet become a fixed component of the ego, pregenital partial drives can be permitted and gratified. In the perversions, for example, repressed drives of a pregenital nature defend themselves successfully against the fate to which the ego has attempted to subject them.

The partial drives, too, in their greater primitiveness, are closely linked with inclinations toward intense aggression. Often their activation is accompanied by an extensive de-fusion of the death and life drives, which are usually bound together. The term *primitiveness* is not meant to imply a moral evaluation here but to refer to early psychological development. The predominance of relatively pure aggressiveness can also be observed in perversions associated with the partial drives; it is such unadulterated aggression that can make these symptoms so dangerous in a person's dealings with others as well as with himself or herself.

According to the American psychoanalyst H. Lichtenstein (1977), the mother, with her care and close contact, does not mold the infant's identity but rather an identity pattern. The drives are built around such patterns, which commence with the early physical relationship between mother and child. This sexuality, which does not serve the purpose of reproduction, awakens the child to life as an individual, to the formation of its own identity. The identity pattern allows for many variations and it is the ability to use its possibilities in a variety of ways, to be able to broaden this identity, that contributes in large measure to the feeling of living a fulfilled life.

I would like to return to the subject of the vicissitudes

of drives and the formation of a conscience or superego. Aggression plays the predominant role in superego formation. With the internalization of paternal prohibitions and strictures, murderous aggression directed against the father is turned inward, toward the ego itself. In consequence, guilt and the unconscious need to punish oneself develop. In order to escape this painful pressure, a person seeks scapegoats, which are used to displace one's own repressed, anxiety-producing aggression outward and project it onto others. For impeded aggression, according to Freud, results in a severe injury to a person, activating the death drive against one's own ego. This model of superego development is, however, applicable only to the male ego.

Erich Fromm (1973) rightly rejected this interpretation of Freud in concluding that Freud's views on the effects of the aggressive and death drives followed the logic of the so-called hydraulic model, which Freud originally applied to the sexual drive. This psychohydraulic model pictures a system of forces or pressures, each linked to the energy of a drive; these forces press unrelentingly for a release of tension. The hydraulic model does apply to the sexuality of men to a point. For women, however, many of whom are frigid today as in the past, such a model cannot be used to explain the origins and functioning of their sexuality.

That physical discharge of the sexual drive is considered necessary for health clearly applies only to men. Some elements of Freud's theory of aggression also appear to be applicable primarily to men. Aggressive forms of discharging drives are regarded as necessary for mental and physical well-being only in men. For women, on the other hand, the repression of aggressive drives and their redirection inward (female masochism) are viewed as the normal outcome of those drives.

Anna Freud (1965) assumed phases of aggression analogous to those of libidinal development; aggression can also be transformed into active forms. Biting, spitting, and ingesting are characteristic of so-called infantile-oral aggression. With toilet training—the anal phase—intense outbreaks of destructive aggressiveness are regarded as normal. People speak of anal sadism when this aggression is directed outward.

During this phase, boys and girls can be observed to display different forms of aggressive behavior, which correspond to their upbringing and socialization; gender-specific differences begin to be exhibited. Boys tend to be permitted more outbreaks of aggression than girls; even at this age, people expect that girls should restrain their aggressive tendencies and begin turning them inward.

The phallic phase is associated with aggressive forms of behavior, such as bossiness, boasting, arrogance, impatience, and rivalrous aggression. This too applies primarily to boys; in girls, penis envy and jealousy supposedly predominate.

According to Spitz ([1965] 1967), Winnicott (1965), and Greenacre (1971), aggression is connected to the need for activity, to self-preservation, and to wishes for mastery in the growing child. One should avoid regarding aggression as merely the expression of hostile behavior and feelings. Lantos (1958) suggested assuming two primary categories of aggression. In contrast to Heinz Hartmann (1964), she doubted the existence of an innate, neutral ego energy not linked to drives. Lantos distinguished between nonhostile destructiveness (comparable to animal forms of aggression such as hunting) and a hostile destructiveness (sadism in the most extreme sense and rivalrous aggression).

Most of these authors stress that not all impeded aggression has self-destructive effects; for example, superego formation generally contributes to the structure of the personality and not to its dissolution. The first forerunners of the superego, namely the internalizations of maternal prohibitions and strictures in early infancy and the development of the ability to say no, serve to neutralize a child's destructiveness and self-destructiveness. The shift from narcissistic to object libido is said to be bound up with a person's psychobiological differentiation; this differentiation has a fundamental influence on the further development of destructiveness. This shift thus initiates the process in which humans are civilized.

Henri Parens (1979) subscribes in great measure to the observations and theories of Margaret Mahler. He holds that phallic aggressiveness is not observed in girls; the first gender-specific differences between boys and girls show up during this phase of development. Thus he would replace the concept of "phallic phase" with the concept of a "first genital phase" in both sexes. The conflicts of ambivalence that are typical at this stage develop (according to Parens) much more intensely in girls than in boys, because a girl's rivalrous aggression is directed toward the mother as the primary love object; that is, the fear of losing an utterly necessary and loved person as a result of her own aggression can be overpowering for a girl. Even before Parens, several psychoanalysts pointed out this conflict-laden situation in girls. Mahler, along with Loewald and other psychoanalysts, viewed the development of aggression as closely connected from the very beginning of life to the behavior of the important primary objects, above all to that of the mother, who is thus made responsible for the early development of aggression.

In my opinion, the vicissitudes of drives are determined from the very onset of life by the people who are close to the child and by their relationships to that child. The behavior of the important primary objects (in our culture this usually means the mother) influences the development of the child's sexual and aggressive drives. But debates continue within psychoanalysis about whether and to what extent the development of drives should be regarded as dependent on object relations from the very first, or whether a primary narcissism predominates at the onset of life. In other words: Does the child perceive its immediate personal relationships from the beginning of life, and does a relationship (of whatever primitive sort) exist between mother and child that influences the development of drives even at this time? Or does the child remain narcissistically oriented toward itself during the first months, remaining at the mercy of the processes associated with its aggressive drives?

I can still remember vividly a dispute between the English psychoanalysts Willi Hoffer and Michael Balint in London during the 1950s. Hoffer (1950) represented the viewpoint (to which Freud was also inclined) that the mental life of all children is dominated by a primary narcissism at the beginning of life. Balint (1952) asserted the existence of a primary love, by which he meant that from birth onward, the infant enters into relationships with the people who are closest to it, and reacts in its own way to their behavior. In the meantime, the so-called psychoanalytic theory of object relations has gained increasing influence; among its advocates are numbered Balint, Winnicott, Loewald, Fairbairn, and many others.

For Freud, the Oedipus complex remained the focal point of psychoanalytic theory; psychoanalysts since Freud have increasingly concerned themselves with the early pre-Oedipal phases of childhood development. If in the past the father-son relationship was regarded as pivotal to an individual's destiny, the relationship to the mother now became the focal point of interest.

Psychoanalysts such as Alice Miller ([1979] 1981) in the German-speaking countries and Jeffrey Masson (1983) in the United States attracted much attention by vehemently rejecting Freud's dualistic theory of drives, and with it the importance of the Oedipal conflict. They claimed that Freud had abandoned the seduction theory as the triggering mechanism of neurotic illnesses, against his better judgment and out of fear of the reaction from society, in favor of a theory of phase-specific Oedipal drive activity and the fantasies and conflicts that correspond to it. This claim in effect calls psychoanalysis itself into question. Every psychoanalyst knows that incestuous seductions or abuses occur in childhood with great frequency and that they can give rise to severe mental and physical illnesses. The point is simply that this has nothing to do with the universal existence of Oedipal fantasies and does not cast doubt upon them. Just as human object relations play a decisive role in the development of drives and the ego from the very onset of life, traumas inflicted by the parents or other persons also have serious consequences, as does childhood seduction. But just what may be considered to be a trauma (that is, a mental wound that causes illness), and when, varies from individual to individual.

Our insane and wicked society is to blame for everything, one often hears. But what is society? Who makes it so evil, so destructive? Such statements ignore the mutual influence that people, states, and societies exert upon one another. Mechanisms of projection and displacement of one's own aggressive needs onto other individuals and peoples are overlooked here as one of the many causes of war or of the mentality of the arms race. Relationships between men and women are also stamped by the different ways in which individuals and society apportion sexuality and aggression with respect to women and men. Surely women are by nature no less sexual or aggressive than men; but they express the needs associated with their drives differently than men. The development of drives is heavily influenced by individual circumstances and conditions in society, as well as by gender-specific experiences.

Psychoanalysts, too, should not lose sight of the interdependence between society and the individual. It is easy to overlook the extent to which fantasies can shape and reshape external reality, on the one hand, and drive-related desires can be guided by traditional social ideas ("constellation of values"), on the other. Repetition compulsions in individuals perpetuate the repetition compulsion of society as a whole. Freud ([1930] 1963) recognized early on the defensive function of prevailing values. By discovering the unconscious motives that lie behind society's illusions, morals, and ideals, he called this constellation of values itself into question, in the hope of freeing humankind from patterns of eternal repetition. "Anyone who panders to prevailing values is in for a rude awakening when in the course of the struggle between classes and parties (from which he remains aloof) victory is achieved by groups with a 'transvaluation of all values' on their agenda," wrote Helmut Dahmer (1983).

I would like next to summarize Freud's theories about female development. In accordance with the patriarchal, phallocentric society in which he lived, he believed that penis envy in a little girl was the prerequisite for her to develop from a little man into a little woman. When a little girl discovers that she possesses no penis of her own, she desires her father's, or a child from him as a substitute, or both. She believes that her mother must hate her because the mother has given birth to a daughter without a penis, and because she is a rival in the struggle for the penis of the father. Penis envy and animosity toward the mother usher in the development of femininity. Thus it is not sexuality but aggression that determines the initial stages of female drive development. A small girl must redirect her aggression inward in order to develop into an adult woman, becoming a masochist in order to be able to enjoy sexual intercourse or even find it bearable. Aggression thus ushers in femininity, and sexuality is more or less abandoned. According to this theory, there are really only two possibilities for a girl: to largely renounce her sexuality and become masochistic or to develop a masculinity complex and persist in clitoral masturbation.

Freud was in a certain sense an ahistorical thinker. He believed that conscious and unconscious childhood experiences determine the course of later life. Human beings all have in common a given complement of drives; how these drives develop depends on the experiences associated with phase-specific object relations. Etiological explanations are the core of psychoanalytic theory and practice. In Freud's works, human history often appears as an eternal repetition of the same; history parallels the history of individuals. Only with the knowledge of the significance of transference and countertransference phenomena was the direct presence of the here and now of social circumstances and their psychic processing incorporated into the analytical process, giving psychoanalysis a historical dimension for the first time.

The view of male and female superego formation presented by psychoanalyst Jeanne Lampl-de Groot (1933) was still essentially based on phase-specific and drive-determined principles. A child's original relationship to the parents is incorporated into the psyche with the help of internalization processes. Introjection is an aggressive process but one that is accompanied by libidinal components. Internalization ensures the continued intrapsychic existence of objects. Passive components of the libido remain uninvolved in the internalization process, according to Lampl-de Groot. Although in her opinion the first developmental phases are identical in both sexes, the Oedipus complex of a girl (which leads to the formation of a superego) is fundamentally distinct from that of a boy. A girl's positive Oedipal posture is a secondary construction, which develops only when the negative Oedipal posture has been abandoned. But the passive components of the libido do not participate in superego formation at all; they remain affectionately attached to the real objects and cause a particularly great dependence on them. Thus, in a purely feminine, wholly passive woman, superego formation does not take place.

In the meantime Lampl-de Groot has advocated a somewhat revised view of the psychosexual development of women. She agrees with many of the viewpoints presented in the volume edited by Harold Blum (1976). None of the authors in this book consider the psychosexual development of women as merely analogous to that of men, and, accordingly, a little girl is not considered to experience herself merely as a castrated little boy. The Oedipal situation is of course influenced by pre-Oedipal developmental experiences, but it is also stamped by upbringing and the attitudes and conventions of the child's environment. Much of the research in this book is devoted to pregenital female identity; direct observations of children, work with transsexuals, and analyses of pregnant women serve as the bases for these studies. The authors arrive at the conclusion that at the beginning of the second year of life, a core gender identity develops. This coincides with the separation from the mother. A child discovers its genitals and prefers playing with them to playing with other parts of the body. Though this cannot yet be characterized as masturbation, it is a decisive step toward the formation of a differentiated bodily image. The separation from the mother can only succeed when the child has accomplished a narcissistic cathexis of its entire body, including the genitals.

The Oedipal phase in a girl can begin only once there is a basis of "primary femininity" (Stoller), that is, the wish for a sexual relationship with the father and a child from him. This phase does not need to be ushered in by a girl's perception of being castrated, as Freud ([1925] 1963) had assumed. In the view of female development expressed in the aforementioned book, there can no longer be any talk at all of penis envy as the "fundamental pillar of femininity." The absence of masturbation during the latency period—which Freud and Lampl-de Groot interpreted as a girl's clinging to her masculinity complex—is regarded by contemporary authors rather as an indication of "genital anesthesia." It is assumed to be obvious that women too can develop adequate ego strength and an integrated sense of self, and that their autonomous female superego enables them to master tasks and crises they encounter throughout their entire lives. Such women can follow their own paths even in a society that on the one hand places a premium on professional advancement, but on the other tends to dismiss a "career woman" as unfeminine. G. R. Ticho (1976) believes that women profit from the current crisis of a rapidly changing world in which notions of value are no longer fixed and that they are able to find new paths to a satisfying, unconventional identity. Blum (1976) also emphasizes that a modern perspective of complete female personality development is represented on the one hand, by pre-Oedipal development of cohesive self and object representations, of identity and gender identity, and on the other, by the post-Oedipal further development of a female and maternal ego ideal. He does not find female masochism in normal women; instead, he regards the capacity to bear suffering as a capability of the female ego, and he distinguishes it from pleasure in pain, or true masochism. According to Blum, anatomy is not destiny, but destiny is what the individual makes out of his or her anatomy.

In the development of human beings, the superego is the most recent psychic authority, and thus more capable of changing than the ego and above all the id. The superego is always the carrier of existing notions of value, in both men and women. Ethical and moral norms that change as society develops also alter the structure and content of the superego. Even so, archaic elements from the first years of life, along with those handed down by tradition, tend to remain intact side by side with new formations.

What changes have taken place in superego formation since the time of Freud? The loss of the father as a recognized authority must necessarily influence the superego in contemporary society. Today the superego of both sexes more frequently exhibits the "double nature" of which Lampl-de Groot speaks, and which she regards as the cause of people's indecisive moral and ethical attitudes; an ego authority of this type is supposedly also less capable of cultural and scientific achievements. I would agree with many analysts that such a "double superego," which is constructed on the basis of internalizations of the father *and* the mother, usually represents a more mature and flexible superego than the kind described by Freud, which is made up exclusively of identifications with unquestioned patriarchal values.

But there is still controversy regarding the content and origins of the female superego, as well as the psychic motives that are decisive for a young girl's switch of objects. Female homosexuality has remained a "dark continent" for many psychoanalysts. Most psychoanalysts are probably little interested in the subject to begin with. Ellen Reinke-Köberer (1978) asserted that within the contemporary psychoanalytic community, Freud's hypotheses about female sexuality are no longer regarded as preliminary but have been elevated to the status of an established and secure theory.

5

Women's Self-Understanding

ACCORDING TO FREUD, the psychic processing of the anatomical difference between the sexes is the source of women's feelings of inferiority and self-contempt. "When she [a little girl] has passed beyond her first attempt at explaining her lack of a penis as being a punishment personal to herself and has realized that the sexual character is a universal one, she begins to share the contempt felt by men for a sex that is the lesser in so important a respect" (Freud [1925] 1963). The little girl now turns away from the mother, whom she experiences as inferior like herself, and feels drawn to a more highly regarded father. Her estrangement from her mother in favor of her father has unmistakable sexual-genital overtones; in our society, this has always been far more acceptable than the relationship between son and mother, which likewise has incestuous significance. It is still regarded as more acceptable for a younger woman to marry a considerably older man than the other way around.

A boy is said to be driven by his castration anxiety to identify with his father (and paternal prohibitions) and to abandon his incestuous ties to his mother. A little girl, who has nothing correspondingly physical to lose and supposedly reconciles herself to this fact in the end, is said to lack the motive for such a severe internalization of rules and prohibitions. That is, she develops a superego that is weak by comparison with a boy's. Even the ability to think in an abstract or precise manner, which has always been considered more the province of men than of women, is said to be related to a boy's rigorous internalizations and more decisive withdrawal from incestuous cathexes.*

According to Freud, any woman who is not prepared to give up her so-called phallic-clitoral sensations will not attain mature genital sexuality. This is supposedly expressed not only in infantile wishes but, following puberty, in the ability to achieve vaginal orgasm. Frigidity and lack of sexual interest in women had been regarded as normal and appropriate to good morals over a long historical period; then attitudes toward female sexuality began to change, partly as a result of psychoanalytic discoveries. The situation was reversed: Any woman not capable of orgasm could not be regarded as normal.

Superficially the situation appeared to be changing dramatically, but, in fact, it was business as usual in many respects. For as women began to subject themselves to the new normative dictate of the vaginal orgasm, they remained at the mercy of men and their preconceptions about "true femininity" despite supposed sexual libera-

*Some years ago various authors (Lowenfeld and Lowenfeld, 1970; Marcuse [1963] 1970; A. Mitscherlich [1963] 1969) pointed out that permissive child rearing, child rearing primarily by women, and the "lack of fathers," that is the lack of a visible paternal model, had led to the superego of the boy being substantially less severe and the sexes becoming increasingly identical in their conduct, clothing, and so forth.

tion. We know that the proportion of frigid women is no smaller today than in Freud's time, but women now suffer from profound feelings of worthlessness associated with frigidity. The research of Masters and Johnson, physiological research on the sexual function, and the experiences of psychoanalysts have amply demonstrated that notions of immature clitoridal and mature vaginal sexuality in women were influenced by the prevailing notions of the times.

Of course it should not be overlooked that universal access to birth control methods means deliverance from anxiety and sexual restrictions for many women. However, the new kinds of relationships that have evolved as a result have very often brought with them new obligations as well, such as the obligation to be always available sexually. With the marketing of the female body and sexuality in general, we have entered a new phase of social attitudes with respect to relations between the sexes. The family has largely lost its significance as the fundamental economic unit of our society. Sexuality is regarded as a marketable consumer product and is fully exploited by contemporary society as such. Thus it is no longer tied to marriage, even for women. Premarital sexual relations are hardly subject to social taboos. By comparison with centuries past, this appears to constitute far-reaching sexual liberation of women.

But we must not overlook the new forms of oppression that come with a new status quo. For example, there is a tendency to impose sanctions against women involved in lesbian relationships. Wantonness, aggression, and criminal activity are imputed to such women (several trials in West Germany in recent years have demonstrated this).

According to still-prevailing patriarchal notions, a "normal" woman has no independent sexuality, or at least none independent of men. Denial of clitoral sexual sensitivity as "male," and the high premium placed on vaginal orgasms as the expression of "mature femininity," are both related to this.

In aligning themselves with the patriarchal ideals of society, women also habitually overvalue sexual love. It is expected that a woman's sole desire will be to be loved, to love a man, to admire him, serve him, and mold herself to him. Such conduct has little to do with women's natural wishes; rather, it is the consequence of an ideal forced upon them, the internalization of which serves primarily the self-regard and sovereignty of men. Only when the heterosexual relationship is held up as the sole meaning of a woman's life in a given society can "typically female" rivalries develop between women.

A further example should help to illustrate the extent to which women's conduct continues to be dictated by men despite women's so-called liberation.

Karin sought psychotherapy because she suffered from depressions. It so happened that, although she was married, she maintained sexual relations with several men; her husband likewise had several girlfriends. She regarded this as normal and progressive.

Her analysis revealed that she was ashamed of nothing so much as her feelings of jealousy; in accordance with the ideals of the male-dominated milieu in which she lived, she experienced her jealousy as the expression of prohibited possessive wishes, and thus strove to disown it at all costs. She could find of no other way to overcome her jealousy than to enter into relationships with other men, provided her husband did not have too many objections—though in truth she regarded his failure to object as a grave insult.

If we look at this woman's childhood, we notice that her father behaved much like her husband: He betrayed her mother with a number of other women, and the mother suffered greatly as a result. In accordance with the customs of her time, however, she was defenseless against her husband's conduct.

Even as a child, Karin was deeply outraged that her mother, whom she very much loved, allowed herself to be so debased by her husband. She thus wished—even as late as the time of her puberty—that her mother would devote herself completely to her and forget the sufferings caused by the father. Nonetheless, she admired her father and identified with many of his qualities and roles, for he had a successful career and was recognized by society.

Karin was also successful in her career. Yet sexually, despite her apparent freedom, she was as dependent as her mother had been on the sexual desires of her husband and the type of conduct prescribed by her peers. Like many women who appear to be nymphomaniacs, she was frigid. Her nymphomaniac, pseudosexual behavior was fundamentally a form of self-degradation and disrupted her sense of self-esteem. She was unable to love and respect herself.

We must assume that the source of this inability was an identification with her father's often despicable attitudes toward women, attitudes that were also shared by her mother. She loved her mother, but the mother's low self-esteem and self-destructive submission to her father offered little encouragement for her daughter to identify with her, even unconsciously. Karin repeated her mother's unfortunate choice of partner when she herself married.

Despite all of the rage and scorn Karin held for her father, he retained his privileged role in the family, especially with the mother; he remained much more important than Karin was conscious of, and played a decisive role in shaping her and her behavior.

But Karin's behavior was more than just a reflection of childhood experiences and an attempt to achieve mastery over them with the help of conflict-ridden, contradictory identifications; to a large extent, her conduct was forged by the ideals and demands of the group around her. She believed that by conforming to the ideals of this group she would gain acceptance, that is, acceptance from the men who shaped it, with whose stipulations the other women, too, were prepared to identify themselves. In so doing she found herself in a hopeless predicament: Because she could not do without the sympathy and support of the others, she destroyed her own sense of self-worth. But the less she respected herself, the more she became dependent on recognition from others. The consequences were depressions and disruptions in her work, which finally drove her to seek psychotherapeutic treatment.

Freud's theories about femininity were challenged not just by feminists but by many psychoanalysts. Among those psychoanalysts who opposed some of Freud's views even as early as the beginning of the 1920s was Karen Horney.

According to Horney, penis envy cannot be explained by the discovery of the anatomical difference between the sexes alone. It originates with the narcissistic overvaluation of the separation process in the anal stage, with the stage of infantile pleasure in seeing others and exhibiting oneself (in which boys are at an advantage), and finally with the realization that boys are permitted, even taught, to touch their penises during urination—something a little girl experiences as permission to masturbate. All of this, according to Horney, leads to an understandable envy of boys and their genital equipment, which a child experiences as more desirable. Infantile penis envy is universally observable, but is of only temporary importance, according to Horney. She was unable to confirm the enduring effects on the later development of women that Freud attributed to penis envy. In her opinion, a neurotic development usually brought on by experiences around the time of the Oedipal conflict was also required for there to be such enduring consequences of penis envy.

What Horney described as secondary penis envy is a form of defense against Oedipal wishes that give rise to anxiety or lead to disappointments. The consequence is that a girl abandons her father as a love object and instead identifies herself with him. It is this identification with the father, inviting invidious comparison by the girl, that allows castration anxiety, wishes for revenge, and feelings of envy toward men to develop, ushering in a girl's phallic stage.

Although Horney's observations are in many respects accurate, in my opinion she underrates the effects on a girl's early development of her parents' tradition-bound, generations-old identifications and notions of value. These influences begin as early as birth, encouraging a little girl to experience her lack of a penis as proof of her inferiority.

Freud first discovered that it is not just external events and experiences that leave their mark on the psyches of human beings and that fantasies also reinterpret external events and create new psychic realities. He subsequently turned his attention to the intrapsychic consequences of

repressed desires and instinctual demands and their consequences for the psychic processing of external reality.
His investigations represented the first time that the unconscious and fantasy became the focus of scientific research on the mental life of human beings. We can hardly
expect that, during this stage of exciting new discoveries,
adequate attention would be paid to the consequences of
differing child-rearing practices on boys and girls or to
cultural attitudes toward women.

Thus, it is also a credit to Karen Horney and other
women psychoanalysts that they focused greater attention
on the importance of external circumstances (i.e., cultural
and social attitudes) for the development of women.

It is important that we strive to understand more precisely how objective events and their subjective psychic
processing are interwoven in people's minds. Analysts are
constantly at pains to make sure that we do not lose sight
of Freud's understanding of the complex, unconscious,
drive-determined, and varied nature of people's psychic
processing of external reality; conversely, newly shaped
psychic realities in turn affect social relationships. But in
so doing, analysts also strive not to underestimate the
tradition-creating power of social organizations and their
effect on the behavior of their members. For it is precisely
because value norms are anchored in the drives of human
beings, or in their repression, that social organizations are
so difficult to change. This in itself is enough to prevent
the legal equality accorded to both sexes from resulting
in real equality. Even in socialist countries, the fact that
women work both on the job and in the family has hardly
changed their low status or the excessive demands made
on them. Without tireless work and until traditional at-

titudes, repressed instinctual demands, and the resulting contempt for women are made conscious, relations between the sexes will never improve.

Freud overlooked, for example, that in our style of child rearing, the male sexual organ is universally understood as a symbol for a more highly valued masculinity; thus it is almost impossible to avoid developing envy toward men. Direct infantile envy of the male genitals, such as can be observed in little girls (and was discussed by Horney), is rarely found in the later life of women. The feelings of inferiority that derive from it remain, along with a denial of one's own femininity.

Feelings of envy for women in men are, of course, quite familiar to psychoanalysts; such feelings include envy of the ability to bear children. This jealousy originates in early childhood and is a consequence of sibling envy and helplessness with respect to a mother who is experienced as omnipotent. But it is even harder for a man to confront himself with his envy of women in a world in which he has learned contempt for women. He thus seeks justification for the anxiety, rage, and aggression toward women that stem from his early childhood and brands them as witches, as loathsome or unscrupulous, or as ridiculous and undependable.

Because women's behavior has changed unmistakably over the course of the last fifty to sixty years, their dependence on similarly evolving social relations should not be overlooked. To regard such dependence exclusively as the result of normal biological and psychological developments is no longer tenable even in psychoanalysis. Our increased understanding of early childhood has also influenced theories about gender-specific development. Freud's theory of psychosexual development has been expanded by the research of Margaret Mahler and her co-workers. Mahler's theories are based on psychoanalytic treatment, direct observation of children, and previous psychoanalytic knowledge; they have gained wide respect for their focus on the types of object relationships that occur during various stages of childhood development. A small child's stepwise dissociation from the mother and individuation make up the core of Mahler's theories (Mahler 1965; 1968; 1972; Mahler, Pine, and Bergmann 1975). In psychic development, they attribute to a phase of rapprochement that begins during the second year an importance as great as that of the Oedipus complex.

I would like to go into this theory in greater detail. According to Mahler, a little girl's turn toward her father is not to be attributed solely to penis envy, even though Mahler and others date awareness of the difference between the sexes to an earlier age than Freud does—to the end of the second year of life. A girl's turn toward her father thus acquires a new significance. The phase of rapprochement is not primarily one of a rivalry conflict in the child, who longs for the parent of the opposite sex and experiences the parent of its own sex as competition, but rather a new step in the development of the child's capacity for individuation. Conflict arises as a result of contradictory needs; the child inherently strives for greater independence but at the same time does not want to leave behind its union with the mother and dependence on her.

The father represents a new object in this pre-Oedipal period of early childhood, one that can offer freedom from an inordinate dependence on the mother. Naturally, the need for a third person is also a reaction to unavoidable disappointments with the mother; but this is not so much a result of penis envy, or of a boy's passive homosexual impulses or a girl's heterosexual ones, as it is a result of the development of a child's normal needs for autonomy. It is only by establishing varying relationships with two people that a child learns to distinguish itself more clearly from its mother and construct distinct self and object representations. E. L. Abelin (1971, 1975), a co-worker of Margaret Mahler, regards this "triangulation" as the third important organizing factor of childhood development (the other two are the capacity to say no, suggested by Spitz, and the ability to walk upright); it may be distinguished from the Oedipal triangle (see also Rotmann, 1978). For it is exactly the close relationship between father and mother that represents the precondition for the child's—boy and girl alike—being able to turn to the father in order to expand the primary mother-child unit. In such an ideal constellation, the result is increasingly what Winnicott (1965, 1971) has described as "cross-identification." A mutuality is achieved in which the parents are able to empathize with their child as well as with each other; the child develops a capacity for differential identification and empathy through step-by-step internalization of this parental behavior.

The problems surrounding the separation and individuation process thus antedate the Oedipal conflict, but they do have a decisive influence on the inception and progress of the Oedipal stage. According to Mahler's observations, the Oedipal conflict can be resolved without an excess of violent aggressions or a rupture in the relationship to one parent only when "triangulation" during the phase of rapprochement has been more or less successful. Penis envy loses its destructive and self-destructive edge, for the child is able to assemble meaningful object representations by internalizing a harmonious relationship to two people who are experienced as different individuals, and can thus develop a coherent self-image. Thereafter, feelings of physical inferiority and fears of being destroyed or destroying others play no further role.

According to psychosexual theory, the mother is a disappointing rival for an Oedipal girl, one who has withheld the penis from her. It is then up to the father to offer a substitute in the form of a child. In addition, the mother is seen as a person incapable of loving her daughter without ambivalence. Mutual empathy plays hardly any role at all here in the tripartite relationship occurring before the stage of Oedipal competition—and this even though Freud emphasized that a man inherits his wife's relationship to her mother. The worse the original symbiotic mother-child-relationship has been, the more urgently the father and later the husband as sexual partner will supposedly be expected to gratify early Oedipal privations. But if the father has shown empathy toward those needs of his daughters that have been frustrated by the mother, this too will supposedly often have a negative impact on a woman's later relationship to a heterosexual partner, at least according to Freud. For in consequence, an inordinately strong, idealized bond to the father may develop, by comparison with which all other relationships will seem disappointing.

But Mahler has a different view: If the separation and individuation phase is completed with optimal empathy for the various and changing needs of the child during separation, triangulation, and rapprochement, the child will also be able to resolve the Oedipal conflict with the help of further developmental stages. The child will be able to preserve its relationship with both parents, whose prohibitions, strictures, roles, and behavior can be internalized, and the child will thus be able to form new ego-broadening identifications.

But all too often, the marriage or household lacks parental empathy and sympathy for the needs of the child. Development of mutual empathy is hampered by centuries-old practices common in our society. Boys and men tend to put their own interests before those of other family members. Fathers often perceive their children as rivals for the attention of their wives, or else side with them against a mother who is felt to be disappointing, omnipotent, or even worthless. Only when both parents are capable of an empathetic relationship with more than one person will they be able to understand the child's dependence and its problems of separation and triangulation.

In various places in his writings, Freud asserted that both sexes develop the need to repeat passive experiences, impressions, and instinctual demands actively in order to finally gain mastery over them. Why should this not be applicable to female sexuality as well? But with women, psychoanalysts regard the need for activity and mastery, so necessary for human development, not as progress but usually as a phallic-regressive disruption. Freud's phallic monism, which rests on the assumption that neither sex is capable of perceiving the difference between the sexes during the first years of life and that both thus experience themselves as small men, has been questioned by a number of psychoanalysts, both male and female. Freud's assumption is contradicted by the observations of Spitz ([1965]

1967) and Mahler (1968). Both boys and girls enter into an original primary identification with a mother who satisfies needs, is idealized, and is active.

The types of behavior and fantasies that led to the assumption of a phallic phase in a little girl often turn out to be the consequence of a traumatic, and therefore repressed, perception of the anatomical difference between the sexes. Exactly when this perception becomes so traumatic that it must be repressed, and whether it activates massive infantile fears of destruction, is something that can be diagnosed only on a case-by-case basis. Inevitable castration anxiety or inescapable knowledge of a female defect are not blanket explanations, since individuals display considerable differences in their psychic processing of this experience.

When a little girl does react traumatically to the sight of the male genitals, the triggering factors may include primal-scene experiences and fear of the effects of her own aggressive impulses. The effects of social gender definitions are manifold; they have a profound impact on the conduct of the mother, indeed of both parents, toward the daughter. Low parental esteem for the little girl, and the different child-rearing practices that go with it, intensify ever-present infantile feelings of ambivalence toward the parents, as well as the little girl's fears of punishment, withdrawal of love, and physical destruction that may accompany these feelings.

The misunderstandings to which psychoanalysis has constantly been subjected make it necessary to add something here that a psychoanalyst would take for granted: Psychoanalysis is concerned with the psychic processing of conflicts associated with primary objects or their internalized representations—conflicts that are played out during the various stages of the development of drives. Psychic conflict in all its possible variations stands at the center of Freud's teaching. But it is with regard to just this point that the so-called revisionists (among whom may be numbered Harry Stack Sullivan and the later Karen Horney) have been much more biological and far less conflict-oriented than Freud; they speak, for example, of "natural femininity," "natural heterosexual powers of attraction," and so forth, while also defining the social preconditions for the development of neuroses far too superficially.

Ernest Jones (1927) agreed with Horney's notion that the phallic phase has a secondary defensive character. For Jones, the phallic phase was not a sign of normal development in either the girl or the boy; it represented instead a neurotic compromise, a defense against the anxiety- and guilt-provoking desires associated with Oedipal drives. Overemphasis of one's own phallic qualities in fantasy life was said to facilitate the warding-off of castration anxieties.

With each stage of psychosexual maturation, the desires associated with primary objects change along with their intrapsychic representations and the types of conflict they engender. The phallic stage of development in a boy is associated with Oedipal desire for the mother; the clitoral-vaginal stage in a girl with desire for the love of the father. Freud was undoubtedly right that we cannot assume that such behavior is ushered in merely by a simple attractive power between the sexes; we must not overlook the fact that these stages also have to do with the complex outcome of gender-specific, pre-Oedipal conflicts in the mother-child relationship.

In summary, it could be said that direct observations of small children demonstrate conclusively that a primary, autoerotic penis envy does exist during the anal stage. But there is also reason to believe that there is such a thing as a primary femininity. Not only does this primary femaleness have biological roots (viz., the present-day recognition of the primacy of female embryo development) but it is preserved in the early somatic ego of the infant that is specifically stimulated by the mother's physical care. Moreover, infants of both sexes enter into a primary identification with an idealized and need-gratifying mother. Unavoidable disappointments with her during the course of development intensify a little girl's need for a new object; the father then takes the place of the idealized love object. If he does not adequately respond to a girl's overtures, or if the mother overreacts to this partial rejection of her, the disappointed or fearful girl very often turns back to the mother, but this time in clear rivalry with the father. That is, the girl defends herself against her own female desires with respect to him by making a phallic identification with him.

It remains an open question whether the original disappointment with the mother can indeed be traced back to the mother's being regarded as that person who has withheld the penis from the girl. Such a disappointment probably does not become manifest unless other disappointments are added or have already been experienced. Prominent among these is the permanent narcissistic disturbance that results from a girl's being less welcome to both parents than a boy.

Yet the significance of ego development in the Oedipal stage should not be overlooked. The ego makes considerable progress during this phase. With this growth comes the ability to distinguish more closely not only between self and object but between object and object. The child is now in a position to establish distinct relationships to two different objects. The child's pleasure with this increased ability to orient itself does not merely lead to conflicts but also brings relief from them and allows the child to distribute and manage them.

A brief survey of psychoanalytic studies of the psychosexual development of women reveals a broader controversy. It has still never been clarified at what point in time a small girl becomes aware of the existence of her vagina. Josine Müller (1931) and Karen Horney ([1923] 1967) regarded it as proven that there is such a thing as a primary sexual excitability of the vagina. Melanie Klein voiced similar views in 1932 (1975), even if, for the time being, she accorded only oral needs to the vagina. Chasseguet-Smirgel, like Melanie Klein, believed that early vaginal drive activity is repressed out of fear of attacks against the inside of the body. She emphasized women's anal-sadistic desires for mastery, which lead to the desire to appropriate the penis vaginally, thereby producing guilt that causes the little girl to repress such needs.

Ernest Jones defended himself in his Vienna lecture (1935) against the objections that the London psychoanalysts accorded too much importance to early fantasy life at the expense of external reality. He claimed "that there is no danger of overlooking external reality, but clearly one of underestimating Freud's teachings about the importance of psychic reality." But, in fact, Melanie Klein, whose views he was defending in this lecture, used words and pictures stemming from the language of adults for a certain "bodythinking," as Fenichel called it, or for pre-verbal fantasies; she thus created the impression that such preverbal fantasies, whose unconscious existence is undeniable, are present in and capable of being verbalized by the child. That a small girl in the first year of life should experience the concrete desire to suckle at her father's penis is not very convincing. That such desires are present and are moreover expressed later, in older children and adult patients, may possibly point to similar preverbal fantasies; this does not suggest, however, that they are actually experienced by a small child.

In addition, I would like to take issue with the supposition that the vagina plays a prominent role as a source of sensations of sexual pleasure in the experience of a prepubescent child. Unlike the clitoris, it only rarely awakens the need to be stimulated by manual masturbation. This does not preclude the fact that the vagina, at least the entrance, is often investigated out of curiosity by a small child, and thus that the existence of a vagina is well perceived at an early age (see Greenacre 1950). I am concerned here only with whether genital-sexual vaginal sensations are generally and intensively experienced before puberty, or whether this occurs only when a sexual seduction has taken place. In this regard, the following discovery of Masters and Johnson (1966) strikes me as interesting: An artificially implanted vagina develops sexual responses similar to those of a normal vagina during the course of sexual relations. Regular intercourse is thus capable of awakening sexual reactions even in an artifical vagina. The two researchers have made similar observations in homosexuals who engaged in regular anal intercourse, and in whom the anus took on quasi-vaginal responses.

In any event, the glans penis and glans clitoris remain the most sensitive sexual organs and demonstrate direct sexual reactions even in childhood. On the basis of these biological facts, I would contest the notions of Melanie Klein and others who assume that the clitoris plays a larger role than the vagina in a small girl only because it provides a defense against fear of the vagina, that is of the inside of the body. According to these analysts, the vagina is the most sexually intensive organ from the very beginning. But it is, in fact, an underdeveloped organ until puberty, with only slight vascular circulation and hardly any secretory capacity. Although they are quite aware of these biological facts, many analysts persist in according the vagina a substantial role in the psychic experience of the child. Thus J. S. Kestenberg (1968) also spoke of an "internal genital phase," in which the internal genital organs are vaguely perceived, that is said to last until a little girl's fourth year of life. Supposedly it is not until then that the clitoris assumes the leading role and the girl begins to deny her femininity and concomitantly her vagina as well.

Melanie Klein ([1932] 1975) and Helene Deutsch (1944) saw the period of devotion to the father and his phallus as the sequel to an original yearning for the mother's breast. The equivalent of male castration anxiety in a woman, according to Klein, is the fear of the interior of the body. As a consequence, and as a result of denials and disappointments (like the mother's breast at an earlier stage), the penis becomes a bad object and is internalized as such. This is said to lead to an early and particularly sadistic superego formation in girls. In order to overcome her fear of this avenging superego, a little girl is said to require external objects more urgently than a little boy, objects that can serve to alleviate her fear of her own guilt feelings and persecution anxieties. In this way she supposedly becomes particularly dependent on other human objects.

In contrast to Freud, who regarded women as having weak superegos, Melanie Klein thus attributed to women a strong, sadistic superego formed early in life. In her experience, a little girl does not suffer from penis envy in the sense of wanting to be a man herself; she merely desires her father's penis, which makes her envious of her mother. A boy is at an advantage with respect to a girl in that he can make himself independent of his mother by virtue of his penis, which enables him to perceive himself as a different sort of being than she is. He supposedly invests his own penis with fantasies of narcissistic omnipotence, whereas a girl can only idealize the introjected penis of her father. Since in her fantasy life she had originally robbed it from her mother, the introjected paternal penis simultaneously aggravates her feelings of guilt.

Chasseguet-Smirgel ([1964] 1970), who is close to the school of Melanie Klein, sees penis envy as a derivative of the omnipotent mother; one can only make oneself independent of her and become her rival when one possesses an organ that she lacks. Chasseguet-Smirgel's interesting interpretation is that the denigration of women shared by both sexes can be traced back exclusively to early fear of and hostility toward an omnipotent mother. Although her observation provides illuminating insight into some individual cases, it seems too one-sided to me. Though there are many plausible thoughts and interpretations, here, as with Melanie Klein, social influences on the parents' behavior toward the child are ignored. All later developments in men and women are essentially projected back onto the earliest mother-child dyad, which is then preserved in the relationship with the father. It is doubtless important to know and be able to evaluate early childhood factors in order to better understand later types of behavior in adults. But when we overlook the role of economic and social factors and their effect on child rearing, we run the risk of regarding the parent-child relationship as though it took place in a vacuum.

I have already referred to the concretizing bodily language used by Melanie Klein. It should be kept in mind that within the framework of her theory, words such as *penis, breast,* etc., are code words for very complex psychic processes. Her notions about "good" and "bad" penises are interesting, for example. With the help of positive partner relationships, a person can overcome an introjected "bad" penis; the penis that was originally stolen from the mother in fantasy can be symbolically given back to her, and guilt feelings with regard to her can be assuaged. In clinical practice, we, in fact, often find that a woman's relationships with her partners of the opposite sex are of a varied nature, and thus do not appear to be directly subject to the repetition compulsion. Freud, who in his later writings described the pre-Oedipal relationship with the mother as definitive for the psychosexual development of women, in the end even came to doubt if his claim that all people experience an Oedipus complex was valid for women, since their ties to the mother were repeated in the relationship with a husband.

Melanie Klein's notions of a good and bad penis can thus add to our understanding in certain clinical experiences in which the sexual partner clearly has not "inherited" an original relationship to the mother. When a woman succeeds in seeing in her partner the embodiment of a good penis, one that helps her to overcome early anxieties of conscience and the feeling of having something dirty, destructive, or stolen inside her, a partner relationship that is wholly different from that with the mother can develop. We frequently find in our practice that a patient's first intensive heterosexual relationship is of a sadomasochistic nature, while a subsequent one is characterized by empathy and mutual satisfaction. According to Melanie Klein, an external sadistic penis, that is, to say the masochistic relationship to a sadistic man, can thus actually be used to destroy the introjected bad penis.

Certainly guilt feelings with regard to the mother (and later with respect to the father) play a role in such a utilization of heterosexual relationships; Chasseguet-Smirgel, for example, has described the influence that such feelings can exert. If the good penis (that is the good relationship to a man) alleviates anxieties related to the interior of the body and guilt, the pleasure gained from the sexual act is doubtless much greater than in situations in which there is mere sexual gratification. In consequence, the alleviation of feelings of anxiety, guilt, and worthlessness provides a fundamental basis for a lasting, satisfying love relationship. The process is aided by the sexual act but extends beyond sexuality. Here it is evident once again that the research of Masters and Johnson relates to only one area of female sexual experience. Their investigations do not take into account the psychic constellations that are essential to a sexual relationship.

We must also concede that Melanie Klein is correct in regarding frigidity in many cases as the expression of an ego's inability to overcome its fears. In such cases, a penis as an external object may unconsciously be just as feared as would be an internal one, so that during sexual intercourse all of the destructive drives and guilt feelings are mobilized at once. This condition of internal anxiety and tension drives many women to seek ever-new sexual relationships. Since these blind attempts to satisfy a drive while simultaneously gaining mastery over anxiety remain trapped in a vicious circle of aggression, fear, and guilt, they tend ultimately to fail.

An example should help to clarify the psychological significance that various partner relationships can have in the life of a woman.

A young woman, Ursula, had been unable to disengage herself from an unhappy relationship for many years because she believed she could neither live with, nor without, the man in question. She finally succeeded in separating, and after about a year became involved in a new relationship in which lasting and satisfying contact developed. What took place here? From the very beginning Ursula had not been able inwardly to approve of her first lover; she could neither respect him nor look up to him as a model. Nor were her sexual relations with him liberating or even very pleasurable—on the contrary, she evaded them from the beginning as shameful, forbidden, onerous, and even nauseating. To all appearances this man had not inherited Ursula's relationship to her mother, for she very much loved and respected her mother. Consciously, at least, she had always gotten along well with her mother and felt herself loved and understood.

However, Ursula had experienced some difficulty with her mother in her early childhood with regard to her sexuality. When the mother noticed that her daughter was masturbating (she was four years old at the time), she made a scene about it. Ursula was taught that something bad had happened, something that would certainly have harmful consequences for her body and mind. In spite of this, she could not entirely give up masturbating, which she increasingly came to regard as a vice. Every time she was unable to resist the need to masturbate, she felt an obligation to go to her mother and confess the latest relapse. Her mother invariably reacted with great sadness and silent reproachful eyes, thereby aggravating Ursula's feeling of having committed a grave offense. Ursula felt unclean and devastated inside, and knew that she had only herself to blame for her misery.

The choice of Ursula's first lover had something to do with her own feelings of inferiority, with her feeling of her own sexual worthlessness. Her partner's "dirty," sadistic penis, which was clearly able to gratify its desires, apparently without guilt feelings, was meant to displace the "bad" penis within her, her own denied sexuality. This of course did not happen, but she was at least freed from the torment of having to cope with her wicked sexuality alone. This sexuality was no longer just an internal factor, but was now out in the open; Ursula separated herself from it when she finally succeeded in separating from her lover. Shortly before that, she had experienced the interruption of a pregnancy. Carrying the pregnancy through to term had been out of the question for her from the start, although her lover would have been only too happy to marry her. Later, during her analysis, she thus experienced no guilt feelings as a result of this experience, although she was usually quite susceptible to such feelings, and a large part of the analysis was concerned with her working through guilt.

By externalizing the "bad" sexuality, the "bad" penis

within her, she became capable of entering into a new and far more positive relationship. The new boyfriend was a person she could respect from the very first. Her sexual relations with him both satisfied and liberated her. She was thus willing to carry a second pregnancy through to term, although external circumstances made this a difficult proposition, and reason alone might have counseled an abortion. In any case, she now succeeded in freeing herself of her deep feelings of worthlessness, from which she had suffered since her early unsuccessful struggles with masturbation. Living together with this lover eliminated her fears of being devastated inside. In many regards he was a respected model for her, one who inspired her. Even so, there were clear differences between this relationship and her relationship with her mother, whom she had also idealized for an extended period of time. She was much more openly aggressive toward her lover than toward her mother; this naturally caused her guilt, but no underlying rage. Her ambivalent feelings toward her lover were thus openly expressed, and not repressed as in her relationship with her mother.

During the course of the analysis Ursula became conscious of how much she had tried to gain her father's love during her Oedipal stage. She retained memories that revealed that it was not just fear of losing her mother's love but also intense disappointment with her father that had driven her to pronounced phallic-exhibitionistic behavior and bound her anew to her mother.

Ursula thus did not repress her anal-sadistic aggression toward her husband in the manner that Chasseguet-Smirgel portrays as typical. Rather, she succeeded in holding in check her destructive impulses of envy and debasement with regard to this "good" object. In so doing, she improved her own sense of self-worth, and the "good penis" in her also made her more generous and patient in her relations with others. In her case, the second lover represented neither the father nor the mother, in my opinion, but rather had an early superego significance, representing a sexuality that the mother too could recognize. Why?

It appeared that the second boyfriend represented her mother's first husband, whom the mother had honored and idealized (in contrast to the patient's father, whom the mother had pitied and even somewhat despised). This meant that now both the originally internalized mother and the actual present-day mother were satisfied with her sexuality, with the "internalized penis." Certainly her sexual problems and the problematic partner relationships that resulted were related to early oral-aggressive and anal-sadistic postures. To this extent, Ursula's confirmed the views of both Freud *and* Melanie Klein, inasmuch as her later sexual relationships had much to do with her earliest experiences and her internalizations, projections, and externalizations of them—even though these sexual relationships did not represent any sort of direct repetition of her relationship to her mother.

If we examine Ursula's history, we find that despite complex intrapsychic processes, it cannot be denied that society-specific child rearing, which determined her attitudes toward sexuality, was an essential ingredient in the development of her problems. Her period of devotion to her father, which might have helped the patient to develop greater independence, was clearly discouraged by her mother; indeed, the mother responded reproachfully as soon as the daughter displayed her inclinations. The father himself was obviously not sufficiently empathetic in his relationship with his daughter, though he admired her. Though she was pretty and a good student, he failed to establish a deeper relationship with her because he was too preoccupied with his own problems and too dependent himself. This hindered the development of the necessary triangulation.

There were only fragments of the sort of bridge between the parents that might have helped the child to expand and emerge from the overly close mother-child relationship. Here one can see that for the daughter's later development, the extent of the father's ability to empathize with the psychic needs of the child was as important as that of her mother. In my opinion, mothers are burdened with far too much responsibility; frequently, this leads to a disruption in the ability of their children, and particularly of their daughters, to individuate.

The disruptions in Ursula's feeling of self-esteem were on the one hand the result of an identification with the mother, who despised herself for her frequently submissive behavior toward the father, and on the other hand the consequence of the more or less open scorn for anything feminine displayed by the father and brother, and shared by the mother. But Ursula's own emotional ambivalence toward both parents produced guilt and led her to question her own worth as a person capable of love and as a sympathetic daughter and woman. If this young woman later repeatedly found herself in similar crisis situations, in which she sought the love of men who were already attached, it was an expression of both her unresolved Oedipal conflict (and the accompanying guilt feelings and tendencies toward self-punishment) and her wish to free herself from an exaggerated dependence on the mother imago. She failed in the latter because in every intimate relationship she repeated the early duality with the mother as well as the wishes for autonomy that stood in conflict with it.

She could be helped in the analysis, however, because the first internalizations of maternal roles in the mother-

child relationship had been largely positive, despite diffi-
culties with separation and the prohibition of sexual autonomy.

She had also been able to integrate later identifications
with the mother, whom on the whole she experienced
positively. This patient had largely been able to overcome
dangerous splittings into good and bad objects, that is the
classification of all her human relationships as either idealized or persecuting, degraded, and debasing. Thus she had
learned to live with ambivalent feelings toward a person
she loved. She was also capable of mourning; meaning
here that she had separated from her own infantile ties
and was enriched and stabilized by the internalization of
a good relationship to a lost object.

Melancholia is produced when the rage intended for an
object that has abandoned a person is internalized and
directed against the ego itself. The "bad introjection,"
that is, the internalization of an object from which separation has taken place and which is degraded and invested
with rage, vengeance, and debasement prevents the ego
from growing with the aid of new and diverse identifications; the person is thereby prevented from maturing. The
consequence is a lasting attitude of reproach accompanied
by unsatisfied dependent needs and self-hatred. Under
such circumstances, the potential for increased autonomy
with age remains undeveloped. Such cases illustrate the
crucial significance of a timely separation, a separation
that does not trigger anger or unmanageable guilt or a
need to be punished. Such a separation is instead encouraged by both parents in order to avoid an impairment
of important relationships. Only under such circumstances
can separations lead to identifications that can enrich the

person, instead of undermining the ego. Melancholia and disruptions in a person's sense of self-esteem are always linked to one another.

Only when the relationship between the parents themselves is free from repetitions of early-childhood egocentric bonding to the mother—that is, only when both are capable of empathetic relationships with more than one person simultaneously—can they understand the child's dependencies as well as its problems of separation and triangulation.

In such relationships, the penis need not become a symbol of both male omnipotence and female inadequacy; nor must it represent a substitute for the mother's breast, satisfying needs for oral gratification. Rather, the penis may be recognized by the girl as an expression of human diversity, symbolizing the capability to enter into new kinds of object relationships. Last but not least, it may ultimately satisfy drive-related needs of a physical nature that are the basis of all heterosexual relationships, without causing loss of self-esteem. Psychic differentiations develop hand in hand with such attitudes; ever finer shades of distinction can be made between object and object and between self and object.

The research of René Spitz ([1965] 1967), Edith Jacobson (1937, 1964), S. Fraiberg (1969), M. Tolpin (1971) and others has also added to our knowledge of early-childhood developments and the evolution of gender-specific types of behavior. A young child adopts its mother's roles, behavior, and ways of reacting by means of numerous small internalizations; these create a basis for its psychic development and represent the beginning of its individuation. The gradually evolving capacity to tolerate temporary physical separation from the mother is the criterion by which one can measure the development of internal autonomy. This itself represents the development of distinct self and object representations, object constancy, and evocative memory capability in the child. When an adequate capacity for separation has been reached, ambivalent feelings can also be tolerated with respect to one and the same person; a splitting into good and bad objects is slowly overcome. This much is clear: Symbiotic wishes for unification with the mother imago persist over a lifetime. Some analysts have thus likened the laborious process of maturation, which stretches over all of the stages of life and is always accompanied by partial abandonment of previous forms of object relationships (and, in consequence, by fear of object loss), to a lifelong mourning process.

As already noted, children of both sexes identify with the mother, whom they experience in early childhood as omnipotent and on whose love they are completely dependent. Skolnikow, Kestenberg, Galenson (1976), Jacobson (1950), and others have reported that both little boys and little girls express fantasies of wanting to have a child. Similar wishes and fantasies are also reported by normal male adolescents. The wish for a child may be observed prior to the wish for a penis; Freud himself reported this. Envy of the ability to give birth and of the mother's breasts, envy of the omnipotent nurturing ability of the mother, as well as the hatred that develops because of total dependence upon her, are said to be present equally in both sexes. And as we have said, Freud ([1905] 1963) noted that the first problem with which a child concerns itself is not the question of the difference between the sexes but the riddle of where children come from.

The stepwise internalization of nurturing, consoling, and protective maternal roles helps a child to overcome its fear, hatred, and helplessness; it also helps boys to be able to behave "paternally" toward children in later life. This was pointed out by Zilboorg as early 1941 (see Zilboorg [1914] 1979).

Our culture still demands that a boy develop particular masculine qualities. He is trained early on to behave in an aggressively self-assertive manner and to suppress his emotions (at least outside of the family). When he seeks consolation from the mother in these struggles he is forced to undertake, she too often tends to respond with a lack of understanding, holding him up to standards of so-called masculinity. Here the need for individuation is given a false impetus, false because it is forced upon the child from the outside in order to promote forms of conduct sanctioned by society. For at the same time, and as a result of gender-specific child rearing, boys are allowed more frequently than girls to indulge in egotistical attitudes. They are not as obliged to sympathize with the needs of other family members, are less often required to help around the house, and so forth.

Greenson (1968) saw a boy's abandonment of his identification with his mother as the precondition for his being able to identify in a normal manner with his father, thus developing a stable gender identity. A gradual separation from the symbiotic relationship with the mother and the turn toward a third person that constitutes the capacity for triangulation in the period of rapprochement must be regarded as the basis for the development of independence in both sexes. The question is whether gender-specific abandonment of identification with the mother, such as those Greenson regards as necessary for a boy, is in fact desirable.

When, in our society, a mother rejects and pushes away a boy, forcing him to behave in a way that many people still regard as masculine, we find all too often that she is traumatically disrupting an important line of identification for him. In so doing, she can aggravate the boy's underlying hatred toward her and later toward all women. This hatred, according to Zilboorg, Chasseguet-Smirgel, and others, has its roots in an early dependence on an omnipotent mother. According to Zilboorg ([1944] 1979), behind deeply rooted fears of the mother of early childhood and a man's underlying animosity toward her (and later toward women in general), however, are hidden projections of murderous wishes toward her, which likewise stem from early childhood.

When individuation, which is the formation of self and object representations, has been more or less successful, a person should also be able to experience his or her body as intact and normal for its gender. Such a positive development depends, however, on the unconscious expectations, ideas, and evaluations that the parents bring to the child. The admiration of the parents is of particular importance in the early transition stages of the first and second year of life, as the research of Margaret Mahler has shown.

A child's most difficult problem is how to combine a variety of role assignments and internalizations into a coherent self-identity. If the mother demonstrates inconsistent behavior, expectations, and values, a little girl will have difficulty in forming a structured, autonomous self-image. One type of frequently observed familial constellation contributes to the difficulty of such a development. This constellation might be briefly summarized as follows: The father, a career man and a representative of society, upon whom the family is economically dependent, is accorded far more prestige in matters of intelligence and social influence than the mother. In this respect he represents an ideal that others strive to attain. Within the family, however, he very often behaves like a spoiled child and is unwilling to place the interests of others above his own, or remains dependent and demanding toward his wife. This tyrannical-infantile side of the father is encouraged by the mother on the one hand but secretly despised by her on the other; her contempt is consciously or unconsciously passed on to the children. Within the family, the mother tends to be the person to whom both father and children turn; they have the feeling that she alone can help when they feel weak and miserable. Outside of the family, however, she rarely holds a position equivalent to that of her husband. In contrast, there is a tendency to ridicule her or even to be ashamed of her in that sphere, even on the part of family members.

Thus we have a mother who on the one hand idealizes all things masculine in identifying with other members of society, and who as a matter of course relinquishes all power outside of the family to the father, but on the other hand, permits him to regress to infantile forms of behavior within the family and in consequence regards him with contempt. Such a mother presents a maturing girl with a perplexing model indeed. For the daughter of such a mother, who might be regarded as typical in our society, soon notices the mother's low regard for all things female, and thus for herself. Often the girl associates this otherwise incomprehensible behavior, which she may perceive only unconsciously, to the anatomical difference between the sexes. But when the daughter then attempts to identify with a more highly esteemed father or brother in order to escape feelings of her own worthlessness, this too is difficult, for she cannot avoid secretly despising the infantile aspects of the father's behavior. She has internalized many of her mother's attitudes and roles in the course of her childhood, and thus, along with the feeling of the second-class nature of her own sex, she also assumes the mother's ambivalent attitude toward the father and the world of men in general. On the one hand, she feels superior to men, on the other hand, she is taught and accepts that as a woman she is incapable of holding her own, that she is hopelessly inferior to men in professional, intellectual, and spiritual life.

A girl's necessary separation from and partial deidealization of her mother, which is facilitated by a turn toward a third person (usually the father), is impeded by this tension between feelings of contempt and idealization with respect to both parents. A child who is unable to separate adequately from the early relationship of duality does not develop an adequate capacity to experience other people as beings distinct from itself. The child thus cannot fully understand that other people may think and feel differently and may have other motivations for their actions and behavior. Such a child will thus find it difficult to empathize with what is unfamiliar in other people.

One could, of course, also interpret typical familial constellations in the manner of Melanie Klein and Chasseguet-Smirgel, regarding them as the consequence of un-resolved anal-sadistic conflicts in the mother and later in the daughter. Guilt feelings develop from sadistically motivated desires to acquire the father's penis or to steal it from the mother in order to assert oneself with respect to an omnipotent mother. The mother, who is in possession of the paternal penis, and later the father or husband, may be idealized as a defense against sadistic wishes provoking anxiety and guilt; masochistic forms of behavior may also develop. One often encounters an "identification with the victim" (the castrated father, the robbed mother) as well, with its accompanying symptoms of self-denigration, feelings of emptiness, and so forth, described by Thomä (1967), Staewen-Haas (1970), and others.

Intrapsychic conflicts do not develop in a vacuum but rather within a human environment. That is, they represent the psychic working-through and internalizations of conscious and unconscious parental behavior, attitudes, models, demands, and projections that, in turn, reflect the power structures and value norms of a given society.

6

Mothers, Fathers, and Partners

ALTHOUGH THE OLD system of primogeniture plays only a minor role in business and politics nowadays, patriarchal structures have to a large extent been preserved within the family. To the outside world, the father is the designated head of the family; within the family, it is the mother who is responsible for seeing to the concerns of the various family members. But the roles of husband and wife have changed as a result of historical factors, and these circumstances have given rise to many of the younger generation's problems with parents.

It is not only factors traceable to individuals that contribute to changing a society. Today the state no longer represents a paternal authority to the extent it once did; we live in a technical and industrial world, an anonymous community led by equally anonymous, technically and industrially trained experts and professional politicians.

Influenced by Freud's psychoanalytic critique of illusions and values as well as by changing trends in his own times, Alexander Mitscherlich wrote *Society Without the*